Henbury Dynasties

D1528666

Henbury Dynasties

MARGUERITE TONKIN

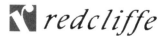 redcliffe

Dedicated to the residents of Henbury,
past, present and future.

First published in 2005 by Redcliffe Press Ltd,
81g Pembroke Road, Bristol BS8 3EA
Telephone 0117 973 7207

ISBN 1 904537 32 4

DESIGNED BY STEPHEN MORRIS COMMUNICATIONS, SMC@FREEUK.COM BRISTOL AND LIVERPOOL
PRINTED BY HOBBS THE PRINTERS LTD, TOTTON, HAMPSHIRE

Contents

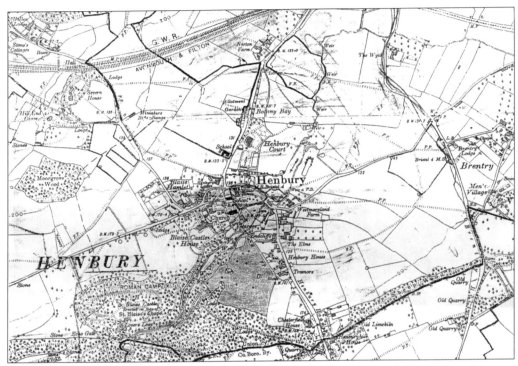

Henbury, a farming village within the county of Gloucestershire until 1935

Introduction

Henbury Dynasties is the third and final book about Henbury by the present author. *Lost Farms of Henbury*, co-authored with Farmer Ray McEwen Smith, looked at three of the ancient farms in the village especially Westmoreland Farm that was forced to cease farming by a compulsory purchase order after the second world war. Norton Farm lost half its acreage in the same way. The smallest of the three, The Elms, continued for another twenty years before relocating. Until redevelopment, Henbury had been a fairly remote village with agriculture its main industry; and in many ways almost self-sufficient. Older living residents remember happily their peaceful country childhood.

Old Henbury looked at the history of the buildings, and traced the origin of the village through archaeological evidence to Neolithic farming communities. It also described village life through the memories of villagers.

As in the above two books *Henbury Dynasties* defines the village as that part of Henbury Parish that lies between the railway line to the north and the top of Henbury hill to the south; and between Brentry hamlet to the east and Blaise Castle park to the west.

Dynasties are seen as families, some of whom lived in the village for many generations, others for one or two generations. All have contributed powerfully to the social and economic life of their community and its ethos. The stories and pictures in the following pages will serve to illustrate their impact on the character of the village.

It is hoped also to show that there was much good will and friendship between different levels of society, between employers and employed. Sadly, this way of life began to change after World War II in a radical way, in parallel with the decline in farming, and the explosion in house building. Some families then moved to areas, mostly in Gloucestershire, that were still rural.

Henbury had not hitherto experienced anything more than a gradual movement of people in and out of the village, largely due to life's altering circumstances. The families included in these pages are among those who stayed long enough to put down roots. In doing so they provided necessary stability to the community, as well as forming a network of neighbours.

This small study is not exhaustive, but it is fairly representative of Henbury families. Those who are included are present through the courtesy of family members who have been willing to contribute recollections of their family life half a century or more ago.

The small trees accompanying most families' stories are there to clarify the text. The more extensive ones have been provided by family members who are themselves researching their family history. The Biggs tree is only a part of the research being carried out by Mr John Roberts whose wife is a Biggs family member. This particular tree includes three families associated with Henbury, as well as with Westbury and Redland.

There are so many themes of interest to explore within the contributors' accounts of their family history. For instance, the Harveys left Devon to find work in hard times, first in Wales, then via Westbury to Henbury. One branch emigrated to Australia, to find land. The Poweslands came to the village because Francis Powesland's employer moved here. Education in Henbury was of a good elementary type. The church schools here also brought the children up in Anglican traditions, thereby maintaining the church as the focus of village life. A few children were able to win scholarships to city grammar schools, sometimes with the aid of the Anthony Edmunds trust. Even greater opportunities lay ahead for their children and grandchildren with the State education revolution throughout the twentieth century.

Some employers and their employees kept up a lifelong friendship and mutual regard long after their working days were over.

Probably some of the most significant changes came from easier public transport, and the telephone. Villagers did not need to be so inter-dependent. World War II finally dispelled any remnant of isolation. With the war over, Henbury's population exploded, whilst many country folk migrated away, so now the special *country* atmosphere is noticed only by those who are in tune with Henbury's past.

The ancient manor house

Ducks and swans on the ford

1

Ancient families closely associated with Henbury through ownership and/or residence

Sadleir, Astry, Farr

It is known from archaeological evidence that farming communities lived in or near Henbury village from Neolithic times. From documented evidence, one learns that in more recent times – AD 692 – Aethelred Saxon king of Mercia, recently converted to Christianity, gave land in Henbury and Aust to the See of Worcester.

Thereafter, for nearly 900 years the Bishops of Worcester owned Henbury. At some date, not presently known, a palace was built to which the bishops would make regular visitations. From day to day, appointees of the bishop would tend the spiritual and practical needs of the people. Estates would be managed and tithes collected. Courts would keep law and order. There would have been many families involved in farming and other food production, and craftsmen such as farriers and smiths. There would have been weavers, thatchers and many other craftsmen and women, and a market to sell their wares.

It may be assumed that there was a small church of Saxon design, and later, a chapel at the palace; but by 1093 a charter makes it clear that a church had been established, probably constructed of stone, for some of the pillar bases in Henbury Parish church are said to date from that period. This can be regarded as evidence of a thriving community of families in the eleventh century. The bishops continued to rule Henbury until the sixteenth century. Various documents throw light on people and events during their ownership, a few of which are mentioned in *A Brief History*.

King Henry VIII removes Henbury from church ownership
After nearly 900 years in church ownership, Henry VIII confiscated Henbury. In 1547 in the reign of Edward VI, it was granted to one of Henry's favourites:

St Mary's Henbury

Sir Ralph Sadleir and his family

The following extracts show how Henbury passed into the ownership of Sir Ralph, and how a later generation disposed of it.

Sir Robert Atkyns

> Henbury was under the authority of Worcester from before the Conquest until Dr Heath alienated his manor and that of Stoke Bishop with the advowson of the vicarage of Henbury to the Crown in 1547 in exchange for some other manors and estates in Herefordshire and Worcestershire.

Rudder: *A New History of Gloucestershire* 1779

> King Edward VI in the first year of his reign gave Bishops Stoke and Henbury in Saltmarsh, and Hundred of Henbury and Advowson of the Vicarage to Ralph Sadleir and his heirs. Thomas Sadleir, son of Rafe was owner in 32nd year of Elizabeth's reign (1590), and left one son Rafe (who had no issue) and one daughter Gertrude who married Sir Walter Aston of Tixal Staffordshire. Their son and heir Walter Lord Aston sold Westbury and Henbury to Thomas Yate and Gregory Gearing on 20th May 1675.

Sir Ralph Sadleir and his family

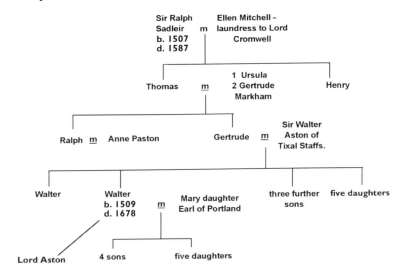

Morse/Astry/Suffolk Family of the Great House

In 1665 George Morse had purchased some land from the Sadleir family, and built a substantial house at the junction of the present Station Road and Henbury Road. In 1675 his son-in-law, Sir Samuel Astry, a wealthy lawyer purchased a large part of Henbury from land agents Thomas Yate and Gregory Gearing. Astry enlarged Morse's Great House and laid out formal gardens. He created a park and planted a double avenue of trees from his house to a summer house at the top of Blaise Hill. Some time after his death in 1698, his widow married Mr Simon Harcourt. (Kip's engraving of the house dates from this time.)

At the death of Lady Astry, and with no male heir, the Estate passed to the three Astry daughters, Elizabeth who was married to J. Smyth, Diana to Richard Orlebar and Arabella to Charles William Earl of Suffolk. Scipio Africanus who died in 1720 was their slave. Arabella and Charles lived at the house between 1715 and 1721 when they both died apparently with no direct heir. The ownership of Henbury was now broken up between the Smyths and part sold. Some of the owners at various times were Edward Colston and heirs, Lord Middleton and heir, and Sir Jarret Smith.

Morse/Astry/Suffolk Family of the Great House

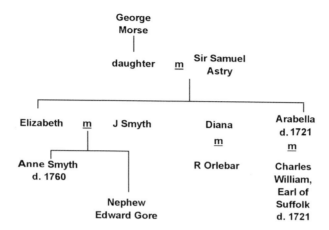

Thomas Farr

In 1762, Thomas Farr purchased the old manor house together with the estate surrounding it. He was a Bristol merchant with sugar investments in the American colonies. He was also a leading citizen, and was made mayor in 1775.

Farr, like Astry, continued to develop his Estate as a private pleasure park, and arranged walks round Blaise hill. In 1766 he famously erected the castle designed by Robert Mylne in gothic style. It was intended as a summer-house to replace Astry's building. (*A Popular Retreat.*)

Thomas Farr lived in the manor house described by Alice Harford:

> The present Dairy garden is on the site of an older house pulled down after the present one (Blaise Castle House) was built. Long and low and gabled, it contained several rooms of fair proportion, and two framed water colours still give an idea of its appearance. The old well is near the water lily pond, and behind the house stood a cedar of Lebanon, in a walled garden.

[Mrs Anne Smyth who died in 1760 had inherited it from her mother Lady Smyth of Ashton, one of the three Astry co-heiresses.]

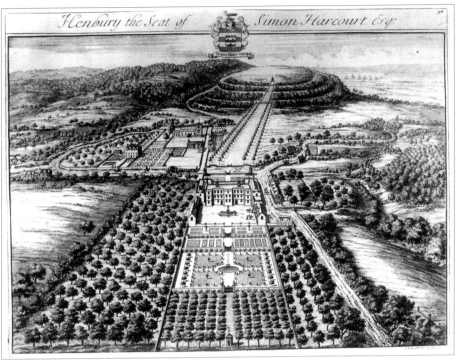

Kip's engraving of the house

Further description of the house comes from *A Popular Retreat*:

> '... essentially a seventeenth century structure but may have incorporated a medieval building. In early eighteenth century bay windows and a porch had been added.'

Unfortunately for Thomas Farr, he was said to be one of many Bristol merchants declared bankrupt in 1778 as a result of the American Wars of Independence.

The newly-named Blaise Castle Estate was sold to a lawyer from Bath, one Denham Skeate.

2

Families who settled in Henbury between the late seventeenth and late nineteenth centuries most of whom remained there for at least one hundred years.

Sampson Way, Way, Harford, Warburton, Baker

In the late seventeenth century, John Sampson from nearby Charlton bought a plot of land in Henbury near to the church. He set about erecting a large house on an earlier building known as Awdelett House. He named the new one, Henbury Awdelett, and completed it by 1688.

Across the Henbury Road stood George Morse's Great House, soon to be enlarged by Morse's son-in-law, Sir Samuel Astry. It seems strange that these two large residences should have been built so close together. It is possible that John Sampson disregarded Morse's house as being too small to signify, and continued his building plans. But, over the years, both houses grew prodigiously!

Henbury Awdelett, later known as the Manor House

The Sampson Family tree

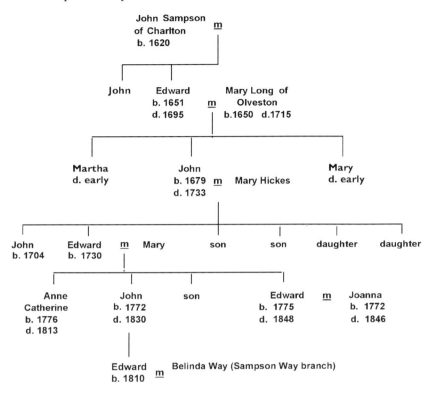

By 1675 most of Henbury had been purchased by Sir Samuel Astry who evidently decided that his father-in-law's house was sited advantageously and appropriately for his own purposes. The majestic avenue of trees he planted from his mansion gates to the top of Blaise hill and the summer house effectively sidelined Henbury Awdelett, and established the pre-eminence of his Great House within the village. However, this pre-eminence was short-lived. By 1760 the Astry property had passed out of the immediate family.

The Sampsons by contrast continued to flourish, and to purchase farmland in Henbury Parish. By at least 1839 when tithing maps were drawn up, they owned, among other farms, the two main village farms, Norton and Westmoreland.

The Sampson Family becomes Sampson Way

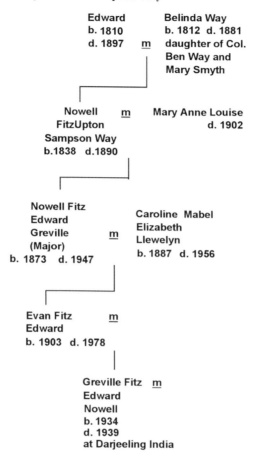

Edward
b. 1810
d. 1897   m   Belinda Way
b. 1812 d. 1881
daughter of Col.
Ben Way and
Mary Smyth

Nowell   m   Mary Anne Louise
FitzUpton   d. 1902
Sampson Way
b.1838 d.1890

Nowell Fitz
Edward
Greville   m   Caroline Mabel
Elizabeth
Llewelyn
(Major)   b. 1887 d. 1956
b. 1873   d. 1947

Evan Fitz   m
Edward
b. 1903 d. 1978

Greville Fitz   m
Edward
Nowell
b. 1934
d. 1939
at Darjeeling India

Then in mid-nineteenth century, they made an interesting marriage alliance with the Way family. This is how it came about. In 1831 Henry Hugh Way succeeded Walter Trevelyan as vicar of St Mary's Henbury. This event was to be the start of an astonishing century of Way ministry in Henbury. Hugh Way had a younger sister Belinda. It is not difficult to imagine how Belinda met Edward Sampson. As a leading village family, the Sampsons would have welcomed and entertained the new vicar and his family. The lane separating the vicarage and Henbury Awdelett is between high stone walls. A garden door into the Sampsons house is almost opposite a driveway into the vicarage. How easy it must have been for the young members of both families to meet!

Within a few years of Revd Way's arrival, Belinda Way and Edward Sampson married. Their son and heir, Nowell Fitzupton was born in 1838, and the family then assumed the surname Sampson Way.

It has been said that the modern Sampson Ways trace their ancestry via the Way alliance (the Ways were related on the maternal side to the Smyth family) to the Earl and Countess of Suffolk. This was not by direct line, I believe, because the Earl and Countess left no heir. The Countess's father owned the Manor and Hundred of Henbury, and so presumably was Lord of that manor. But as we have seen, their family ownership had ceased by 1760.

In the years that followed, the Blaise section was sold separately, and other numerous plots for the building of large houses, including John Sampson's Henbury Awdelett. His descendants bought up farmland in Henbury. It is also possible that they purchased the title 'Lord of the Manor', or they may have acquired it by inheritance. This may explain why Henbury Awdelett became known as 'Henbury Manor'.

Belinda and Edward's son General Nowell Fitzupton Sampson Way died in 1926 at a ripe old age. Tom Hignell remembers that his father Clem took over the lease of Norton Farm from him in 1917. At that time, the General was a widower of many years standing, and was living at Berwick Lodge, thus leaving the 'manor house' to his son, the Major, and his family.

In 1931, Ray McEwen Smith took the lease of Westmoreland Farm from the Major who had inherited his father's Estate in 1926. Ray's grandfather William had rented the farm from the General, and Robert McEwen, Ray's great grandfather had leased the farm from Edward Sampson.

In a previous book, it is explained that Ray McEwen Smith was entrusted at the early age of eighteen years by Major Sampson Way with the lease of his farm. Ray describes there how the farmers went up to Henbury Awdelett to see the Major every Quarter Day to discuss repairs and rent review. While awaiting their interview, they were served a glass of sherry. Ray remarked that he always found the Major very fair even though the rent seemed to rise and rise rather too frequently!

It was the death of the Major in 1947 that precipitated the compulsory purchase of Henbury's farmlands by Bristol City Council.

Way family: a clerical dynasty in Henbury

In 1727 a new vicarage was built near the church overlooking the Dell and the brook. A number of incumbents successively made their home there including the naturalist Walter Trevelyan. Following Trevelyan the Reverend Henry Hugh Way became vicar of Henbury in 1830. He was the son of Ben Way of Denham Place, Buckinghamshire, and Mary, daughter of Thomas and Jane Smyth.

Henry Hugh had 4 sons and four daughters. The eldest, John Hugh, born 1834 followed his father as the next vicar of Henbury.

John Hugh had 3 sons and a daughter. His third son Charles Parry Way,

Golden Wedding Day 1911: Rev. Canon JH Way, his wife and family

The Way Family tree

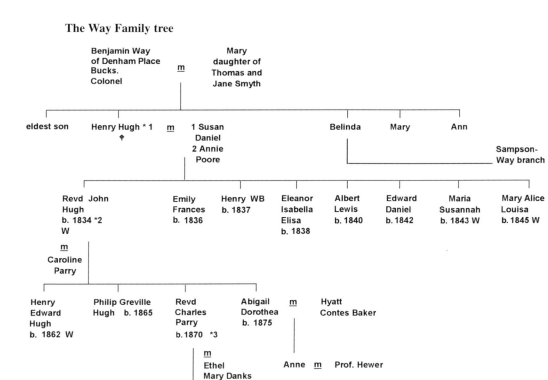

† **Buried Henbury churchyard**   *1. Vicar 1830-1860   *2. Vicar 1860-1906   *3. Vicar 1906-1928

born 1870, followed family tradition and became vicar of Henbury in 1906.

For almost a century from 1830 until 1927 the Way family lived at the vicarage. That they adored their home and found peace in the house and garden is evident in *A Memory of Henbury Vicarage 1830-1927* by C.P. Way.

To return to Henry Hugh, his household was already large with eight children but Henry Hugh and his wife had their aunt Anne Way living there too. Two romances took place in their family, the first, already noted, was Belinda's marriage to their neighbour, Edward Sampson. Belinda was Henry Hugh's sister, but Susan Way also had a sister Louisa who found happiness in Henbury, for she married Revd Walker Gray who was Henry Hugh's curate.

C.P. Way writes in his *Memory* that the Bristol Riots occurred during his grandfather's incumbency, and that H.H. rode over to Ashton Court returning with pockets and saddlebags stuffed with family jewels. Years later, his little grandson was led to searching parts of the garden hoping to disinter the Treasure!

Canon and Mrs CP Way

> It was Henry Hugh who had the tunnel made under the vicarage garden, helped by the gifts of various friends. Before this was done, a right of way passed over the grounds….through the yard by the front door… C.P. Way writes. …In the house itself during his time, the lower kitchen was added and the back staircase to the lobby…..probably also the aviary and arbour on the terrace.

Some accounts of Henbury have the vicarage dating from 1727. However, C.P. Way believes a vicarage on the same site had been rebuilt and altered over the centuries. He writes that Revd John Gardner, Vicar 1730-1779, seems to have made many changes reconstructing a very large part of the building, so that the house which Henry Hugh knew is a house of long passages and many doors, and nooks, and corners, an ideal home for children's romps and games, as also is the garden with its terraces and slopes

The Vicarage

The Dell with the wild cherry in bloom

and multitude of lurking places. In 1860 when his son became vicar, Henry Hugh retired to Alderbourne Manor, Gerards Cross, Bucks.

John Hugh had in 1861 married Caroline Parry, daughter of Admiral Sir Edward Parry, the Arctic navigator. They and their four children lived together in peace and happiness until John Hugh's death in 1912. During their tenure, the stables and gardener's house were replaced. He used to ride about the Severn Marsh on his mare, Erin, the gift of his father. He and his wife would ride out in a quaint basket carriage or four-wheeler behind the ponies Topsy and Rex. Then there was the high dog-cart he drove with a perilously loose rein.

The children enjoyed many pets – dogs, cats, squirrels, rabbits, guinea pigs and dormice, magpies, canaries, pigeons. They had a joyful country childhood as may be imagined, located as they were in close proximity to the Blaise Castle woods with the stream running at the end of their garden. C.P. Way remembers

> the swing near the Gazebo …Rounders and Bowls on the tennis courts …thrilling games of Hide and Seek along the top of the Rock, and Red Indian hunts through the recesses of the wood. ..He tells about the Dell having a peculiar charm with its primroses, anemones and daffodils, wild cherry blossom and hawthorn each in its season.

And the Hazel Brook was a source of great fun, though even in those days, parents were very doubtful about 'stirring up the water'. Nevertheless Harry Way launched his rocking boat on the stream with disastrous results. Hugh pursued nasty vermin (water voles) with catapult and pistol. Andrew and Abigail lured a bridegroom into a home-made and dangerous craft on the morning of his wedding day. C.P. himself as a child fell off the ladder bridge, and frequently paddled in the cleaner pools. In those days too, Councillors and Surveyors wandered up and down the banks devising schemes to restrain its wild and wintry waters.

The family had many friends and neighbours in the village. They also had loyal employees. Frederick Wakefield is mentioned, the gardener who lived in the old stablehouse, and who 'for many years, helped only by a boy, attended to garden, lawns, pony, cows, pigs and fowls – until at last my father was able to give additional help.'

The creation of the Easter Door between vicarage and church has a moving origin – when John Hugh died, his wife remained in the vicarage with her son and his family. C.P. Way, in conjunction with his aunt Mrs Gore-Joyce, had it made to give his mother easy access to the churchyard. It was through this door that she was carried to the church 'through the radiancy of the setting sun' to rest for the night before her funeral.

C.P. Way left the vicarage in 1927 in the belief that, during their family's residence there, the house had been consecrated by prayer and hospitality to the service of the parishioners of Henbury, and that around it has been that atmosphere of loving kindness and sympathy that should always be the chief treasure of a country vicarage.

Harford Family of Blaise Castle Estate
Motto: Inter utrumque Tene (keep the golden mean)

The family descends from the Harfords of Marshfield in Gloucestershire. Alice Harford writes that her family definitely takes descent from Charles Harvorde or Harford of Bristol who was baptized 17.5.1621, and died 6.12.1709.

After four generations well-endowed with sons and daughters, John Scandrett Harford was born in 1754, taking his middle name from his mother's family.

J.S. Harford I
John's son, also called John, describes his father as upright and honourable, beloved by his children, warm-hearted, and generous to his quietly-given charities. 'His was a cheerful and joyous nature, kept under due control, with a fund of quiet humour, and amusing anecdotes. He had great confidence in his wife's judgement, frequently consulting her, and ever honouring her by word and deed in the presence of her children.'

There were nine children, five of whom lived to a good age. A notable exception was Eliza, their third child who died when very young of a fever that also nearly killed her father. Their writings express their profound grief, and also their deep devotion and faith; their joy of living and their depths of sorrow.

John and Mary lived a quiet life due, it is said, partly from a natural inclination and partly from Quaker isolation. They all took great pleasure in riding for itself, and as a means of enjoying the countryside. Almost every year, they drove in their carriage on a leisurely progress through beautiful parts of England such as the Lakes, Devon and Dorset, Kent and Sussex, South Wales, Oxford and Blenheim. Dawlish and Weymouth were often visited for sea-bathing.

John and Mary started their married life in Brunswick Square where most of their children were born. John's father had helped found the Harford Bank, and John became a Partner, remaining there until his death. He was also very involved with the great city guild, The Society of Merchant Venturers, becoming Warden in 1782, and Master in 1798.

After his near-fatal fever in 1789, John rented Knole Park near Almondsbury where they all stayed for twelve months. While there, John made a final offer of £11,000 for the Blaise Castle Estate, the Inn and the Blacksmith's shop. It was accepted by the owner, Denham Skeate.

John Harford did not care for the 'manor house', so he decided to start again, and commissioned William Paty to build a residence to replace it. The house was begun in 1795, roof completed in 1796, and furnishings were complete and ready for habitation in October 1798. Then the 'manor house' was demolished.

Humphry Repton was engaged by Harford to improve the Estate. Repton was a leading exponent of the 'Picturesque' school, and in the Blaise Estate, he had a most appropriate subject. It was Repton who designed and engineered the driveway from his Tudor-style lodge through woods and gorge to the house. Woodland, gorge, rocky outcrops and 'the hill' must have been a joy to work with!

The 'new house' as described by Alice Harford,

The Corner House and Post Office built by the Harfords on the site of the ancient inn

> ...had walls two feet thick, and measured 66ft by nearly 58ft without
> the long wing of the offices or the Picture Room (1832/33). The warm
> orange of the stonework and the beautiful classical proportions...have
> a marvellously fine effect against the green slopes of turf, and rich
> variety of tint and shape ...of the trees.

Inside, the finely proportioned staircase had graceful balustrades of wrought iron. The hall and portico were floored with Portland stone, which had come round by sea.

Humphry Repton's plan to add dignity to the house was to build the cellars above ground with earth heaped up to the level of their roofs forming a gradual slope in every direction from the terraces. By 1798 the family was installed, and took great joy in supervising the continued building operations. Paty designed the stables but, dying soon after this, the work was continued by the architect, John Nash, who then designed the Dairy near the site of the demolished 'manor house'. The conservatory was finished by the autumn of 1806.

Mindful of their large staff, Harford purchased a plot of land across the Kings Weston Road, and Nash designed nine cottages and, with the collaboration of George Repton (son of Humphry) these were set round a green and water pump in 'Picturesque' style. Although designed as a unit with common features, each house was unique. In this model hamlet for their employees, each house had a privy, oven and washing copper, and were modern in their time.

Harford's house in its landscaped environment was fitly complemented by pastureland where he kept sheep and dairy cattle, viewed from the house across a ha-ha. From early days, a bailiff managed control of stock and sale of produce.

John S Harford II DCL FRS

John S. Harford died aged 61, and was succeeded by his eldest son – John Scandrett Harford II.

J.S. Harford II inherited the Blaise Castle Estate in 1815, bringing his own style to the interior of the house. He had been able to travel to Italy about the time of his father's death, in the peace following the Napoleonic wars. He and his wife Louisa collected statues and pictures. This influence can be seen in the classical friezes in hall and dining room, also the Lorenzo de Medici cast in a niche in the hall. His major contribution to the house was the Picture Room placed between house and conservatory. For this, he employed C.R. Cockerell who shared his classical interests.

They also added the colonnade of columns in front of the garden entrance, also a terrace balustrade and classical urns. There were also interior additions to library and upstairs corridor, and general plasterwork.

John and Louisa spent a long and happy life in their house; at least, in their portraits they look happy. John died in 1866 aged 81, and Louisa six years later, 60 years after her marriage to John. They had no children of their own but relationships with family members were excellent. Alice Harford, from whose book most of the above material has been derived, writes,

> ...all the nephews and nieces on both sides, with their children found in her a loving sympathy for their various joys and sorrows. In her widowhood, she gathered together the records of their past life, adding such notes as she thought needful.

John Battersby Harford

This John was the son of Abraham Gray Harford-Battersby who had taken the name and arms of Battersby by Royal Licence in 1815 in accordance with the Will of his cousin William Battersby. Abraham was the second son of J.S. Harford I. This branch of the family owned an Estate in Wales which John Battersby Harford had inherited from his father at the age of 32 in 1851. Fifteen years later, he inherited the Blaise Estate from his uncle J.S. Harford II. Nine years later, he too died leaving a widow Mary, two sons and six daughters.

Falcondale the country estate near Lampeter appears to have remained the principal residence, but for many years Mary (daughter of Baron de Bunsen) lived at Blaise Castle House as a widow with some of her daughters until her death in 1919. Seven years later, her son sold house and estate to Bristol City Council. Mary Harford's tenure there was remembered with appreciation by some of Henbury's older residents.

Alice, one of Mary's daughters, writes of the way her father improved dwellings and living conditions of his tenants in Wales, of developing the town of Lampeter, and his wife's principle of absolute religious equality in their dealings with everyone. An example of his philanthropy was when in 1868 he set aside a field on the Westbury side of Henbury Hill to be used as allotments by Westbury villagers. Three acres and a cow each for his farm labourers was another of his schemes.

His daughter describes the home life, 'so peaceable and idyllic' that it seemed to the children the most natural thing in the world, and they only grew to realize in later life that it arose from the rare and perfect harmony between their parents. Their father always welcomed his children's companionship whether shooting, riding, fishing or overlooking the estate work and farm and cottage repairs.

The Harford Family tree

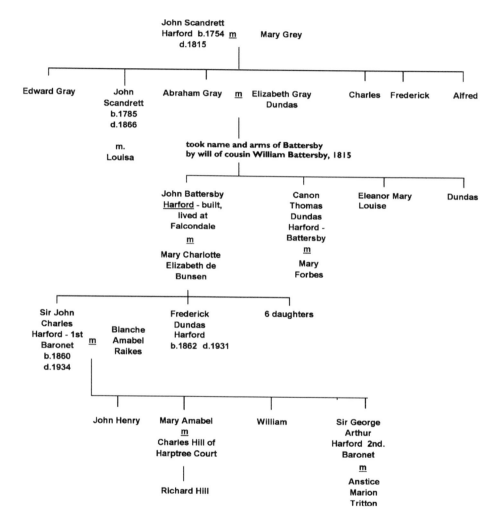

John Scandrett Harford b.1754 <u>m</u> Mary Grey
d.1815

Edward Gray

John Scandrett b.1785 d.1866

m. Louisa

Abraham Gray <u>m</u> Elizabeth Gray Dundas

Charles   Frederick   Alfred

took name and arms of Battersby by will of cousin William Battersby, 1815

John Battersby Harford - built, lived at Falcondale

<u>m</u>

Mary Charlotte Elizabeth de Bunsen

Canon Thomas Dundas Harford - Battersby

<u>m</u>

Mary Forbes

Eleanor Mary Louise

Dundas

Sir John Charles Harford - 1st Baronet b.1860 d.1934

<u>m</u> Blanche Amabel Raikes

Frederick Dundas Harford b.1862 d.1931

6 daughters

John Henry

Mary Amabel

<u>m</u>

Charles Hill of Harptree Court

Richard Hill

William

Sir George Arthur Harford 2nd. Baronet

<u>m</u>

Anstice Marion Tritton

During Mary Harford's occupation of Blaise Castle House, the Castle Inn was taken down. This is the notable inn where J.S. I had with the 70 labourers celebrated the roofing of his house. It was demolished, it was said, to widen the road for 'the easier passage of her carriage'. In place of the Inn, a new post office and corner house were erected. The corner house became the home of Mr Jarrett the bailiff, and his wife who ran the Dairy.

Older residents remember Mary Harford's many acts of kindness, a few of which are described below.

One day, when Mary Harford was out in Blaise woods in her carriage, she met a young mother returning to her family after the early demise of her husband. On hearing her story Mrs Harford offered her the use of one of the cottages in the Hamlet in which to bring up her children. Eventually, the mother went to work in the laundry of Blaise House. Milk from the Dairy was free to villagers who could not afford to pay. Mary and her daughters used to visit the Hamlet via the tunnel to assure herself of the well-being of her employees.

There seems to have been a consensus of opinion that the Harford family were good and philanthropic people. In the particular ethos of their time, they were very much appreciated.

Mr Richard Hill, grandson of Sir John Charles Harford first baronet, who was the eldest son of John Battersby Harford, remembers his grandfather as 'indeed a kindly man'.

He also sent a note about the Society of Merchant Venturers:

> I had understood that the Society of Merchant Venturers of the City of Bristol received the Royal Charter from Edward VI in 1552. This gave it immense power and influence far beyond the City of Bristol, and links were made with other Livery Companies. Had it been only a 'City Guild', as you have called it, the official history as written by Patrick McGrath would have been different, and the City Council might have treated the S M V with less favour and respect. S M V was a City Guild in origin!

Warburton / Stevens / Hellen Family of Henbury Post Office

John Warburton was appointed to be Sub Post Master of Henbury on the thirty first of July 1857 at a salary of £3.10 per year, increased to £7 in September 1857, plus £10 for the delivery duties. He first had his grocer shop and Post Office in one of the cottages (demolished 1890/93) between the wall bordering the road opposite the Hallen turning, and the high wall backing Blaise House lawn. He lived there with his wife Mary and their family.

In about 1890 the Harfords demolished the Castle Inn, and replaced it with the Corner House and Post Office. John and his wife, Mary, then moved into the new premises, and by 1891 at latest, their daughter Sarah and her three children were there also. (Sarah's husband Harry Stevens seems to have disappeared some time earlier.) John Warburton had retired by then, and was succeeded by his daughter as sub-postmistress. Sarah's daughter Edith was her assistant, and her son Joseph at 16 years of age was rural postman. Daughter Margaret at twelve was still at school.

Joseph Stevens

At the age of 24, Joseph married Kate Stockden, a farmer's daughter from Olveston. The wedding reception was held at New Passage Hotel. They then went to live at Oak Cottage, Blaise Hamlet, the only tenants at that time who were not connected with the Blaise Estate. The rent was £5 a year, rising to £6.10 shillings in December 1920. Oak Cottage was then thatched. All their water was drawn from the pump in the centre of the 'green'.

They carried it home and kept it in an earthenware jar in the stone scullery; a tin mug was hung nearby for drinking and filling the kettle. This spring water was very hard, and not much use for washing as it curdled when soap was added. So rain water was collected from the roof into large water butts – the water was tinged brown from the thatch! Lighting was supplied by oil lamps and candles, and cooking was on a coal-fired range. There was no bathroom, just a copper, and an outside privy.

Joseph and Kate's three children, Maurice, Marjorie and Violet were born at Oak Cottage. Maurice in his old age reminisced to Ray Govier about his

The Warburton / Stevens / Hellen Family tree

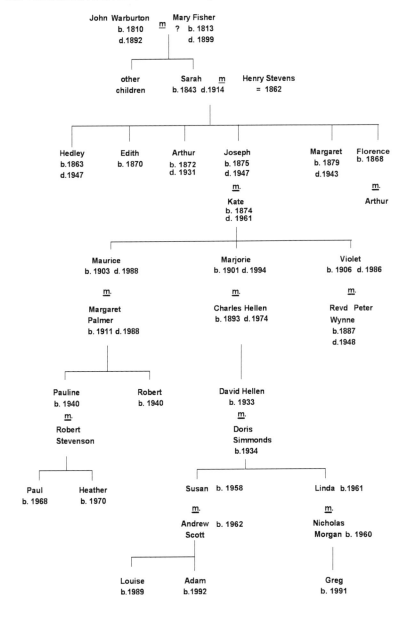

John Warburton
b. 1810
d.1892

m

Mary Fisher
? b. 1813
d. 1899

other children

Sarah
b. 1843 d.1914

m

Henry Stevens
= 1862

Hedley
b.1863
d.1947

Edith
b. 1870

Arthur
b. 1872
d. 1931

Joseph
b. 1875
d. 1947

m.

Kate
b. 1874
d. 1961

Margaret
b. 1879
d.1943

Florence
b. 1868

m.

Arthur

Maurice
b. 1903 d. 1988

m.

Margaret
Palmer
b. 1911 d.1988

Marjorie
b. 1901 d. 1994

m.

Charles Hellen
b. 1893 d. 1974

Violet
b. 1906 d. 1986

m.

Revd Peter
Wynne
b.1887
d.1948

Pauline
b. 1940
m.
Robert
Stevenson

Robert
b. 1940

David Hellen
b. 1933
m.
Doris
Simmonds
b.1934

Paul
b. 1968

Heather
b. 1970

Susan b. 1958

m.

Andrew b. 1962
Scott

Linda b.1961

m.

Nicholas
Morgan b. 1960

Louise
b.1989

Adam
b.1992

Greg
b. 1991

country childhood:

> Our childhood seemed to be full of excitement, wandering in the nearby fields, Moore Field, Long Field, Style Acre and the Steeps, picking the wild flowers, bird-nesting, and collecting hazel nuts in Moorgrove Wood. There was a pond in every field which was always a great attraction. My sister fell in the 6-acre pond, and a pal of mine, the son of the police sergeant slipped into the Moorgrove pond, and as he had his winter coat on at the time, by the time we got him out, his coat was so heavy with water that he struggled home with some difficulty.

Maurice, Kate, Joe, Marjorie and Violet

> One of the high spots for us children was when the Green was cut; we could hear the men sharpening their scythes very early in the morning. I have a photograph of us playing in the hay. This would have been about 1912. Then we took our tea into the adjoining 6-acre field, and we always, I remember, had gooseberry jam.

Joseph and his family left Oak Cottage in 1927 when they bought Corner House next to the village post office for £400. By that time, Joe's sister Margaret had followed her mother, Sarah as sub-postmistress, having been appointed in 1909. In 1925 she bought the Post Office from Major John Harford for £500. When the telephone kiosk was erected in 1923 in front of the Post Office, permission had to be obtained from J C Harford. Until then the public phone was in Telephone Cottage.

In 1935 Joseph retired from his job as Postman, with many accolades from neighbours and clients, and continued to live next door to his sister at the

Joe's café on Church Lane

post office. But Joseph was far from idle in retirement. His grand-daughter Pauline writes about him:

In 1933 Joe Stevens opened the café in the former Reading Room, located behind the Post Office and next to his house, and opening onto Church Lane. He and Kate served teas, and ice-cream and sweets, and later on cigarettes. It was well-known, and people would walk through the woods to sample the home-made jam. They had many regular customers. Joe used to cut the bread wafer-thin in the back-kitchen of his house, then the teas were carried from his yard across the garden and into the café. I can remember too, the days of cutting up Walls ice-cream blocks before the days of wrapped ices, and putting wafers round the slices. On hot days it used to melt all over the chopping board! At Bank holidays, special buses brought visitors to Blaise from Westbury. They formed queues down Church Lane in the evenings (outside the café), to go home, so this was very good for the sale of ices and sweets! I think this must have been in the early fifties.

David Hellen also remembers his grandfather Joe Stevens in the kitchen of his house slicing bread, and warming the butter in front of the range, 'Tea served, being a pot of tea, and bread and butter and jam.' David also remembers that Joe had an allotment on the Hallen Road, 100 yards below the hamlet, where David spent some time with his grandfather. Later, in 1944, Joe bought a plot where number 11 Kings Weston Road is now sited, and they moved the apple trees in a wheelbarrow from the old allotment to the newly-purchased land.

Joseph and Kate's daughter Marjorie married Charles Hellen who had a grocery business in Westbury on Trym. After the death of her aunt Margaret, Marjorie in 1943 took over the running of Henbury Post Office as Sub Postmistress at a salary of £158 per year. Marjorie and Charles had one son David, who was ten years old at the time they moved into the Post

Office. David delivered telegrams when not at school. Marjorie finally retired from the Post Office in 1969 – a total of 112 years' service for the four Sub Postmasters and later, in 1978, she went to live in the Corner House. Her retirement closed a dynasty of service to the village, a dynasty that facilitated contacts between Henbury people and the outside world in an era before rapid and mass communication.

Joe Stevens about 1933

Joseph and Kate's daughter Violet

The present generations know little about Violet, the third child of Joseph and Kate. What small amount is known has been collected together by her niece Pauline Stevenson as follows:

Violet was born in 1905, a pretty child with lovely auburn hair. She grew up and married a curate, Revd Peter Wynne, in about 1936. He was very much her senior, and died in 1948. She set off for Scotland to be a house-keeper in a nurses' home, and then later in hotels around Scotland. This she continued to do for the rest of her life. She married George Moncrieff, a chef, but the marriage did not work out very well. So she continued her work, and died in Scotland in 1986. She was very smart, always wearing her best clothes. She had no children.

Joseph and Kate's son Maurice

Maurice's daughter Pauline writes

> My father was born, and grew up at Oak Cottage, later moving with his family to the Corner House. He was a pupil at the Boys School (Antony Edmonds') in Henbury until he was 13 years old when he left to take a job as office boy at Chittening ammunitions factory. In 1918

Margaret Stevens, Marjorie Hellen, Kate and her sister Emily. Café garden 1950

when the factory closed, he joined the meat importers, Thos. Borthwick and Sons at Old Market Street, Bristol as an accounts clerk. He remained there all his working life. He did not really care for office work but this was a steady job in uncertain times.

In 1939 he married Margaret Frances Palmer at St Alban's Parish Church in Westbury Park. Born in Brislington, Margaret had spent nearly all her life until marriage in Westbury Park. She and Maurice settled down in a newly-built house in Reedley Road, Westbury on Trym where they lived for the rest of their lives. In 1940 their twins, Robert and Pauline were born.

When war came, Maurice was not accepted for national service because he had an enlarged heart. He was very upset to learn this fearing he would not live to see his children grow up.

He grew very proficient at his accounting work, and could add columns of figures faster than an adding machine. In his quiet way, he was popular, well-liked for himself and for his humour, including verbal jokes and 'Heath Robinson' devices.

Apart from his family and his job, Maurice had many interests. He was creative, making book-cases and a chest of drawers. His grandchildren were delighted with the rabbit hutch he made for them, doll's house furniture and little wooden cars.

When his father Joseph died in 1946, he left the café to Maurice who ran it at weekends himself. During the week, my mother went to open it with the help of one employee. I spent most of my childhood weekends in Henbury either helping in the café or sitting with my grandmother, Kate.

About 1962 the café was rented to hairdressers, and the shop was moved to the front room of the Corner House after my grandmother had died.

Maurice Stevens in 1933

It was Maurice's interest in local history that has provided many insights into the village of his birth for the benefit of future generations. With Ray Govier, another local historian, he made tapes of his memories that have been transcribed and stored at Blaise Castle House museum.

Maurice and his wife both died in 1988, she from a massive stroke, he from many small strokes, but humorous to the last.

Maurice's twin children, born 1940
Born and brought up in Reedley Road, Westbury on Trym, Robert attended Q E H School, then went up to Pembroke College, Cambridge to read Classics before becoming a schoolteacher. Pauline, after schooling at Redland High School and O-levels, worked as a laboratory assistant at Long Ashton Research Station.

Robert so far has remained a bachelor, but Pauline married Robert Stevenson who is a chemical engineer. Their two children, Paul and Heather have MSc degrees in, respectively, geology and biological science.

David Hellen is the son of Marjorie, Joseph's daughter. David writes,

Maurice on one of his twenty motorcycles

I arrived at Henbury Post Office in 1943 when I was aged ten. My father had a grocery shop in Westbury on Trym, and I still attended Westbury Park School until I was eleven, then went on to Cotham Grammar School.

I got to know the local Henbury boys through Choir and Guild. We would 'go down the Rec.' (Arthur Baker Memorial Ground in Station Road), having a go on the swings, or just being boys. (The apples in the orchard behind Henbury Lodge were particularly good.) We watched the Cricket Match, Optimists shared the Ground with Henbury. I remember Ike Cox, groundsman, Fred Jefferies who was a big hitter and Mr Tom Broad.

Then we helped with the hay-making. I was once asked by Tom Hignell to go and fetch the large wooden hay rake from the rickyard opposite Norton farm.

Or we would go 'up Blaise'…..had to keep out of the way of the Park Ranger while we climbed trees, floated sticks in the stream etc. The ponds at the Dingle end of the woods were full of water at that time, and we enjoyed frightening each other in the tunnel that the stream goes through at the back of one of the ponds (or Lily Ponds as they were known.) Later, I recall the upheaval when sewers for the new housing estate were laid through the valley beside the Hen, as we then knew it. A lot of Polish workers helped with this.

David's co-adventurers at that time were, from the hamlet, Robin Broad, Gordon, Donald and Royston Dance, Jonathan and Ian Pollard, Michael White from Rock House, Brian Frost from Chesterfield House, and, from Ison Hill, the Steer brothers, Bob and Gordon and Percy and Jack Furber.

The Guild (Henbury Young Communicants Guild), church based and run by Mrs IE Ubank of Passage Road, was very popular – the only activity in the village for teenagers. They had weekly meetings. In the summer, there were such events as paper-chasing, treasure hunts, picnics, walks; and in winter – dance lessons, speakers, amateur dramatics. Members were expected to attend Communion Service the first Sunday in the month – another gathering-together of friends from Henbury, Hallen, Brentry, Cribbs, Lawrence Weston etc. At Christmas, they had a trip to the Pantomime, and on Bank Holidays, a coach trip to such places as Whipsnade Zoo and the Isle of Wight. On another occasion, they all cycled to Aust, left their bikes at the farm just across the road from the ferry, then across the Severn, and walked to Tintern.

Soon after his move to Henbury, and acquiring a bike, David started delivering telegrams after school and during holidays and weekends. He explains,

> There were no official Telegram boys at Sub Post Offices, but the 'ad hoc' deliverers were paid. Telegrams would be phoned through from Bristol, and then the deliveries 'took off'. The delivery area was : Top of Henbury Hill, Crow Lane, through Brentry to the top of Black Horse Hill, Compton Greenfield, through Hallen, part way to Severn Beach, back to Chittening, the farm below Lawrence Weston and the village itself, and as far as the Lodge at the Henbury end of Kings Weston (where Fred Talbot lived), and back to Henbury.

There were two areas that David was not at all keen to visit on his delivery trips, they concerned geese and Lawrence Weston House.

> Several of the farms had a flock of geese wandering about the yard,

and you always had to go round the back of the house to find someone because the front door was never used, and inevitably the geese would approach. I found them very sinister for they would come towards you and hiss, and it wasn't any use trying to shoo them away. I preferred dogs to those wretched birds!

Lawrence Weston House has gone now. It used to be on the right as you went down Lawrence Weston Road from Kings Weston Road just opposite to where there was a bit of a quarry, and where some town houses have now been built. And the grounds of the house itself have now been built over, It must have been a fine house with great views. I don't know the history of it at all, but it was then unoccupied. It had been slightly vandalized, and the house, presumably the back of it was very close to the road so that as you cycled by, any of the ghosts (someone had assured me it was haunted) could just reach out of the glass-less windows, and grab you!

I hated delivering to Lawrence Weston, and would cycle by as fast as I could with my head down. Later, the house was inhabited again, this time I believe by a Mr Allen who had a motor car business in the city.

David grew up and married Doris Simmonds. They live not far from Henbury, in Stoke Bishop. David and Doris have two daughters, Susan and Linda. Susan married Andrew Scott, and they have a daughter, Louise and a son Adam. Linda married Nicholas Morgan, and they have a son Greg. Louise, Adam and Greg are seven generations from John War-burton, their great, great, great, great grandfather who originated the dynasty that provided the once isolated Gloucestershire village of Henbury with a most vital connection to the outside world.

There is no longer a Post Office in the heart of the old village. The premises are now run as a small general store. The Reading Room/Café has been delightfully restored, and is used as a private residence. Nowadays, most people have telephones, cars, the Internet – communication is infinitely easier. Henbury as a suburb of Bristol is well-connected to other suburbs and to the City Centre. But, in its day, Henbury Post Office was indispensable to its residents, both rich and poor.

Baker Family of Henbury Hill House

To pre-war Henbury schoolboys, the Arthur Baker Memorial Ground was known as the 'Rec'. That was where they played football and had fun together. That was where the Henbury Robins started. The piece of land was given to the Parish in memory of Arthur Baker by his widow. After the war, and the massive land development, it was incorporated into the grounds of Henbury School. Few of those boys in later life knew much about their benefactor, only, perhaps that he lived in Henbury Hill House. He would undoubtedly have been pleased that his 'Rec' was so popular with Henbury children because children's welfare was close to the heart of this eminent and philanthropic citizen of Bristol.

Until very recently, the only information to come to hand about Mr Baker was included in the WI book, *A Guide To Henbury*. In the paragraph about Henbury Hill House is the following:

> ...For many years in the last [19th.] century it belonged to Arthur Baker, a corn-merchant, who used to ride on horse-back from his home to his mills on Redcliffe Back.
>
> His family gave Henbury the recreation ground in Station Road which bears his name.

Recent information came from Mr David Culliford, a close friend of Mr Peter Powesland (lately, sadly, deceased.) Peter had found and purchased in a second-hand shop, a handsome leather-bound book of obituary notices that someone had carefully and beautifully compiled. 'Arthur Baker' is printed in gold on the cover, and inside it is possible to learn a little of Arthur Baker's wide-spread interests.

There are also notes that Peter made, and correspondence, all of which throw more light on this eminent man's life. It seems that, in 1995, Mr Geoffrey Baker from Maine USA got in touch with Peter during a visit to Britain in search of his ancestral home. Information and pictures were exchanged, and Mr Baker and his wife went to look at Henbury Hill House.

From gravestones in the upper churchyard of St Mary's Henbury, and elsewhere, one learns that Arthur Baker was born in 1841, and came to

The Baker Family tree

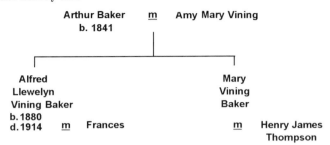

Arthur Baker   **m**   Amy Mary Vining
b. 1841

Alfred Llewelyn Vining Baker b.1880 d.1914   **m**   Frances

Mary Vining Baker   **m**   Henry James Thompson

Henbury in 1881. He and his wife had at least one son and one daughter. His wife had been born Amy Mary Vining, eldest daughter of Joseph Vining of Bristol and Banwell. Their son Alfred Llewellyn Vining Baker was born in 1880 and died in 1914.

Peter Powesland writes,

> I am not sure how Alfred fits into the family but I know from an old minute book that his widow Frances served on a committee formed in 1923 to discuss the family's offer to donate a recreation ground to the parish. In 1924 she was its chairman. I find from an old list of names and addresses that in 1925 she was living at Vine House (then called Endcliffe) together with a Miss N B Thompson, possibly her sister. One of the gravestones testifies that Mrs Llewellyn Baker, as she seems to have been styled when she was a widow died as Mrs Harrison. As I understand it, she married the local schoolmaster Mr Harrison who was secretary to the recreation ground committee when she was its chairman. I was told by an old Henbury resident that after the marriage in about 1925 they left the district.

The gravestone inscriptions also include Archibald Henry James Thompson and Mary Vining Thompson, probably the son-in-law and daughter of Arthur and Amy Mary Baker. Peter comments,

> In 1964 I bought, in the same second-hand bookshop in which I found the Arthur Baker obituaries, a collection of various pamphlets and articles about the history of Henbury and Westbury on Trym bound together in one volume. Between the pages, there were letters and notes addressed to Mr Hamilton Thompson who presumably owned

Henbury Hill House. The gardens leading to the Broad Walk and *below* the drawing room with 'D' window

the book. In 1925 he was listed as Professor A Hamilton Thompson M. A .D. Litt. F. S. A., living at Beck Cottage, Adel, Leeds. I think but cannot give evidence to support my belief that Hamilton Thompson lived at Endcliffe at the time of the first world war.

Before her marriage, Mrs Baker was Amy Mary Vining, and her brother the Revd FW Vining conducted the graveside part of A.B.'s funeral service. Canon Leslie Gordon Vining, born 1885, was Vicar of St Alban's Westbury Park in Bristol from 1918 to 1938. He became Archbishop of West Africa, and died in Freetown, Sierra Leone in 1955. He too may be related.

The Obituaries

These are numerous, and indicate the breadth and depth of this man's responsibilities and interests covering four main areas, his business life, civic, philanthropic and religious commitments. There are indeed so many of these that a representative sample must suffice at this present time.

> In business, he was a corn merchant, starting as a founder/partner in a small private Company that eventually amalgamated with Spiller and Company. He became Director for nineteen years, thirteen of which he was Chairman of Directors. He was also a member of the Bristol Docks Committee.

> In his civic duties, he served as Sheriff in 1891, and as a J.P. from 1887. He was a member of Committee at Bristol General Hospital, and of the Girls Penitentiary.

> His favourite interest seems to have been in education, and he was governor of at least the Redcliffe schools, Bristol Grammar School and Colstons. He took a keen interest in the life of these schools, and worked hard in their favour.

This remarkable man comes across the pages as someone who cared for people and for their well being. So perhaps it is not surprising to learn that he was a truly devout person. His first love (in churches) was St Mary Redcliffe where he was at one time Churchwarden, and to which he made gifts of an altar cloth and windows. But he was also loyal to his parish church of St Mary in Henbury where he regularly attended early communion service on Sundays.

He died suddenly in 1909 at the age of sixty-eight years. His funeral was held privately at St Mary's Henbury attended by family, close friends and villagers. Simultaneously, there was a service of thanksgiving at that other St Mary's at Redcliffe. It was said that the same hymns were sung at both churches.

Only two generations of the Baker family lived in Henbury, covering a span of about fifty years. The 'Rec' is no longer there in Station Road. It is sad that such a man as Arthur Baker should have left so small a memory in his village of Henbury. Perhaps his descendant, Mr Geoffrey Baker will be remembered in Maine, many years after his demise!

Note:
David Culliford has pointed out that nowadays there is a patch of grassland within the grounds of Henbury School that is reserved as a children's play area – perhaps this is a remaining vestige of Arthur Baker's 'Rec.'?

3

Country families born and bred
Woodsford/Talbot, Love, Painter and Clifford

This section is about country families who were very involved in rural ways, and to a large extent were content with their lifestyle. They found employment within Henbury's great houses, respecting their employers and for the most part, looking on them as friends: Woodsford/Talbot, Love, Painter, Clifford.

Woodsford/Talbot

For many years, Mrs Woodsford lived as a widow at number 3 Botany Bay Cottages. Her son Wallace married a Westbury girl, Winnie Malpass at Westbury on Trym Parish Church. At first the young couple lived with Wally's mother, later moving to number 13 Botany Bay Cottages, Station Road.

As a young girl, Winnie was in service at Budgetts of Tramore. She had one day off a month when she took her wages home to her family. Living in, she started as under-maid, and did such chores as black-leading grates. Later, as a married woman, she eventually became Nanny to the Budgett children, when she was always called 'Woodsford'.

Her husband, Wallace, known to many as 'Wally', had become chauffeur to Mr Gunn of Henbury House at just turned seventeen. One outstanding occasion was the day that he took the Gunns' daughter Diana to be presented to King George V. He recalled that there was a long queue of cars at the Palace, so he had to drive round and round the Palace forecourt until their turn came to drive up to the door! The Gunns were good employers, and would even lend Wally's family a car for their holidays.

Wally played for the Hallen and Henbury Football Association, and this must partly explain his interest in and support of (together with Mrs Gunn) the Henbury Robins Boys Football Team. 'Henbury Robins' was a group of local boys who gathered together on the Arthur Baker Memorial

Ground. They were very keen young footballers, but needed some adult support. This was provided by Mrs Gunn and Wally Woodsford. Mrs Gunn arranged for the boys' football shirts to be washed for matches, and she and Wally each drove a carload of boys to away matches.

Wally's colleagues were his brother Albert Woodsford who was the Gunns' gardener, and A. Williams. Frank Powesland who was Dr Wills's chauffeur was a friend of Wally's. Later on, Mr Woodsford became chief mechanic to Stan Biggs after Stan's milk delivery carts became a mechanized fleet.

Wally and his wife Winnie had two daughters and one son. The daughters were Denise Elizabeth (Betty) and Catherine Joyce (always called Joyce), to whom Mrs Budgett became godmother. Betty was born at no.13 Botany Bay Cottages, Station Road. Like all her friends, she started school at the Infants class at Station Road School, progressing to the Girls School in the same building. She left school at the then newly raised school leaving age of fifteen. Her special friend was Mary Baguley (sister of Peter, and the daughter of Church Sexton Baguley), who lived at Sextons Cottage just beyond the church gates, in Church Close.

Betty also had a somewhat older friend Annie Goodfield who used to look after her when she was little. Annie lived next door with her family at number 14 Station Road Cottages. They had fun playing on the street, walking in Blaise woods, sometimes helping at Norton Farm. Betty remembers fetching milk from Hignells (Norton) farm in a jug. She also recalls the Porter Stores when it was an old country pub. It had wooden benches round the back of the bar and yard. Older residents remember when the Windsors' sweet shop and cobblers occupied what later became the saloon bar of the 'Blaise Inn' (previously Porter Stores). For children between the wars, this sweet shop, as may be imagined, was well-frequented!

All the Woodsford family attended St Mary's Church, and Betty went to Sunday School, and later to Communicants Guild. In about 1939 the family moved over Henbury Hill to Hillsdon Road.

Betty grew up, and married Fred Talbot.

The Woodsford Family tree

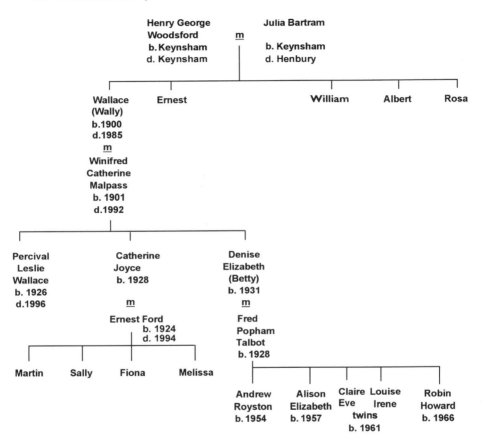

Fred was born at nearby Charlton Village. His family moved to Avonmouth, then settled in Henbury Lodge, Kings Weston Road. He remembers that they paid rent of £6 twice a year for the Lodge in 1939.

Fred writes that his father was sidesman at St Mary's Church Henbury. Both parents walked to church every week mainly to Evensong. Fred himself combined duty as a Server with membership of the 'great' choir – sixteen boys and eight men with Mr Ransome as organist. Fred ended up as head choirboy after Peter Powesland. He writes,

I attended Henbury Boys School when Mr Smart was Head Master. At

13 Botany Bay Cottages

Wallace and Winifred with
four generations of
Woodsfords

Henbury United 1920-21.
Wallace Woodsford standing left

The Talbot Family tree

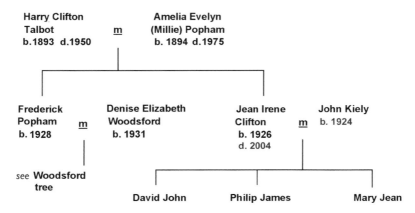

that time, there was no upper floor in the school building. Entering through the front door, the existing reception area was then the large classroom. Then the large main high hall was partitioned, and held three classes. The lavatories were outside. The present car park was part play ground (near the school) and part allotments.

At eleven years of age, I started at Bristol Cathedral School. After leaving school, I was apprenticed in engineering and became Fitter and Turner at British Oil and Cake Mills, formerly John Robinson and Co. in Avonmouth. I subsequently entered their Drawing Office as Designer Draughtsman.

Betty and Fred had five children, Andrew, Alison, twins Claire and Louise, and Robin. After living in nearby Brentry for many years, Fred and Betty retired to Devon.

The Love Family of Brentry, Hallen and Henbury

On 29th July 1916, at the age of 35, Charles Love was killed in action on the Somme. He lies buried in the London Cemetery, at Longueval in France. Following his death his widow Ann was left alone to bring up four young sons – Ted, Arthur, George and William. They lived at 6 Berkeley Cottages in Charlton Lane, Brentry, which at that time was surrounded by beautiful countryside and farmland.

The gardens of Berkeley cottages backed onto the extensive grounds of Hodges Nurseries. To the east was Panes farm on Fishpool Hill. There was Jo Rowles' farm, and the fields of Mr Farr, of Brentry Lodge. To serve this farming hamlet, the Miss Dunsfords kept a small general store and post office on Passage Road. Close by were more cottages including Harry Hignell's house and dairy. The Crow Inn at that time was a private house.

Granny Love with George, Ted and Bill

In this peaceful environment the Love boys were raised by their mother to be honest, upright and hardworking.

Ted Love, the eldest child

He was at the tender age of eleven when he assumed his

Berkeley Cottages

position as head of the family, taking responsibility for the care of his mother and younger brothers. They were a close, loving family and to this day Bill reminisces of the bond between the brothers and how proud he was to have Ted as a brother. Though only a child Ted obtained work at Biggs' Dairy, seeking permission from his headmaster to arrive late in the mornings in order that he could help with the milking. His mother 'took in' washing for the Sampson Ways of the Manor House in order to supplement Ted's earnings.

Ted started as a general farm worker, haymaking, and moving cattle. On one occasion, when moving the bull, held by a ring in the bull's nose

The Love Family tree

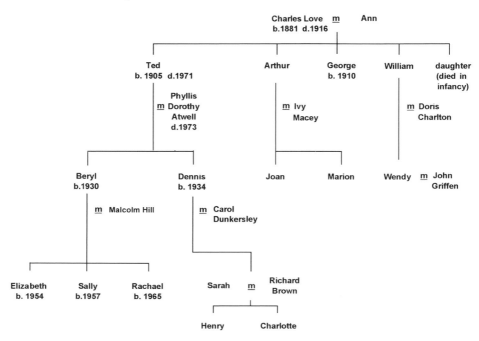

attached to a long pole, he caught his arm between the pole and the farm gate – resulting in a serious arm injury. It was, at times, dangerous work! At haymaking time, the men would often work for as long as the natural light allowed, and then sleep amid the hay bales in the barns and eat provisions sent across by Mrs Biggs. After leaving school Ted continued to work at The Elms until retirement.

Later on Ted became a milk roundsman driving a horse-drawn trap containing a churn of milk and a ladle. Customers would come out of their houses with a jug which was filled by the ladle. He also drove the trap to neighbouring villages even as far as Cheltenham Road; and delivery was twice daily. Later, milk bottles became the norm, and by 1930 milk and other dairy produce was delivered by motorised vans.

While Ted was growing up, he had plenty of good friends and neighbours including the Croker family, Jim, Lena and Vera, also Buller and Ted. Buller

Croker was a life-long friend of Ted Love from schooldays and through their working life at Biggs' Farm. With some of his young friends, Ted would sledge down Knowle Lane Hill in wintertime, sweeping round into Charlton Lane. When the Lily Pond on Ray Smith's farm froze over the friends enjoyed skating on it. However, one of his friends came to near-disaster there. Ted's favourite pastime was running. He was a founder member of Westbury on Trym Harriers. Originally, members would meet by the White Lion having changed into their-running clothes on what is now the Primary School's playing field. None of their

Granny Love with Ted and Phyllis

Four generations: Ann Love, Ted Love, Beryl Hill and Elizabeth Hill

belongings was ever guarded, and none was ever stolen. Ted went on to be a champion, winning many medals and prizes.

In his early twenties, he met and fell in love with Phyllis Dorothy Attwell who lived in College Road, Westbury on Trym. The house stood were the modern houses now are at the top (church) end of the road. They married at Westbury Parish Church and made their first home in Moorhouse Lane, Hallen. Between them, they had many friends and relatives in Westbury, Henbury, Hallen, Brentry, and further afield. Although Westbury had been annexed by Bristol in 1904, all the others were still Gloucestershire villages. Farming communities were interconnected, and many were intermarried.

Granny Love and her sons   Ted and Beryl at Weston-super-Mare

In 1930 their daughter Beryl was born followed, in 1934, by their son Dennis. By this time they had moved from Moorhouse Lane to 2 Blaise Hamlet – the 'Green' as it was then called. Beryl and Dennis attended Henbury Infants School in Station Road (which stood where the new Henbury School is now) and then later Henbury Girls and Henbury Boys Schools. Beryl recalls that during air raids the children and local residents would hurry to the shelter in the Blaise Castle Estate, the entrance close to where the children's play area is today.

Eventually, the family moved back to Berkeley Cottages with Granny Love. Ted and Phyllis remained in this house for the rest of their lives.

Church played a big part in everyone's lives. On Sundays the children went with their parents to the morning service at St Mary's Church and then on to Sunday School in the afternoon – sometimes followed by Bible Class before returning to church for Evensong.

When Beryl reached the age of 14 she left school and went to work in Mills the grocery store in Westbury. At 15, Dennis left school to serve an apprenticeship as a draughtsman at Rolls Royce and Bristol Aircraft Corporation (now BAe).

Beryl remembers,

Dennis, Beryl and Ted outside 6 Berkeley Cottages

> I believe Granny Love was instrumental in getting the cottage on the 'Green' for us, and I have clear and happy memories of living there. Joan Early would take me to school, it was Joan's grandfather who was responsible for collecting the rent from the Hamlet residents.

Beryl continues,

> I cannot remember exactly when we moved to Berkeley Cottages but understand that the move was made to support and care for Granny Love as she became older. My memories of Berkeley Cottages are also happy ones. Granny would take me to the Methodist Chapel in Knowle Lane, then, after the Service, we would walk with friends to Charlton Village, passing Panes Farm and down Fish Pool Hill. At the Methodist Chapel service Stanley Mealing would read to us and on occasions we would have to read to the congregation from the pulpit, which was quite an ordeal! We attended Mr Phillips in Dragonswell Road for Bible lessons. I also attended St Mary's Church in Henbury village. Life was very different then. Every year on Ascension Day we would take part in a ceremony called 'clipping the church'.

Dennis recalls,

> We would all attend Ascension Day service then go outside and, holding hands, encircle the church. Once the circle was complete we would sing the hymn 'We love this Place, oh God'. All the children would then be allowed to play for the rest of the day.

School Sports' Day, the 440 yards

War-time: 1939-1945

Dennis has written a few anecdotes about Henbury in wartime.

> Hodges Nursery, behind the gardens of Berkeley Cottages employed casual labour, amongst whom were German prisoners of war. One, whom we nicknamed 'Fritz', used to call at the cottages trying to sell items he had made. I remember my mother buying a pair of rope slippers from him. As I recall, they were very well made.
>
> At my school, we had a chap named Graeme Hodge, a relative of the Thornes of Hallen, who came here from his home in Jersey to avoid the German invasion.
>
> During the war a small light aircraft was forced to land in the field opposite Ray Smith's farmhouse in Crow Lane.
>
> We had Anderson Shelters in the gardens, one shelter for two cottages. We shared ours with Annie Croker and her father who had difficulty walking, and he used walking sticks. One night, the air raid warning was rather late, and bombs were dropping before any warning was sounded. We all rushed to the shelter. However, we were all beaten to it by old Mr Croker who was first in, without sticks – self-preservation I

suppose! Some of our other neighbours and friends were Alice, Jim and Nick Robbins, Mr and Mrs Morgan, Joyce and John, and the Offers – Emmy, Dot, Aubrey and Maurice.

Beryl recalls,

Ted and Phyllis by the Anderson Shelter

John Morgan was a lovely boy and a great friend, it came as a terrible shock to us all when he was killed in the War. I can still hear Mrs Morgan's cry as the news of her beloved son's death was broken to her.

Ted Love's Brothers, Arthur, George and William

Charles Love's second son Arthur completed an apprenticeship, and then decided to take his skills, and seek his fortune in Australia. Ted saw Arthur to the train. It was a tearful occasion for a close family. At the last moment, Ted gave his brother an envelope, he had collected all the money he had, to help his brother make the best possible start in his new life. There was very little money but it was a huge gesture and typical of Ted's generous and selfless nature. Arthur settled down and married in Australia. He and his wife had two daughters, Joan and Marion. The families kept in touch for years, but with the passage of time, contact was lost, and attempts to make contact again in recent years have been without success.

George was Charles Love's third son. During his childhood George spent much of his time with his Aunt Rose and her husband George Smith, who ran a farm on land which is now tennis courts, just off Cranbrook Road. On leaving school George applied to be an apprentice at BAC (now British Aerospace), and stayed with the company until his retirement at the age of 62. He married Ivy Macey from Westbury on Trym whose father was a prominent businessman, a coal merchant and founder-member of the Men's Club. They had no children but lived happily in Eastfield Road. Ivy died in 1987, George in 1999 after a long retirement. Both Beryl and Dennis remember a story told to them about George: 'When the 1914-18 War Memorial was built in St Mary's churchyard, George Love and Gwen Stevens (a girl from Fish Pool Hill) both had their names put in a bottle with a number of coins of the realm for that period. This 'time capsule' lies buried under the foundation stone of the War Memorial.'

William was the youngest of the four brothers.
When Bill left school, his first job was as a gardener for Silvey's in Cribbs Causeway. He then obtained employment with Bristol City Council. During World War II he served as sergeant in the Royal Military Police near Yeovil. After the war, he returned to Bristol Council, working as school caretaker, first at Penpole School then at the larger Portway School, both in Shirehampton. He married Doris Charlton, and they had one daughter Wendy, who now lives in Nottingham.

All the Love boys were athletic but Ted and Bill particularly so. Bill was involved with the Hallen and Henbury Football Association; he distinguished himself playing hockey for the Army, then, after the War, cricket and golf became his sporting passions. Bill was a member and one-time captain of the Henbury Robins. He recalled that Mrs Gunn was their sponsor and bought much of their sports equipment. She would allow her chauffeur to drive them to matches.

In December 1992 Bill and his wife Doris went to live near their daughter in Nottingham. Just six weeks later Doris died sudenly. Bill went on to build a life alone and made many friends. He had great joy from his grandchildren and great children. Bill died in 2004.

Ted himself retired at the age of 65, to live only one more year, dying of cancer in 1971. His wife Phyllis died two years later.

Ted Love acted as father to his own father's family. He was adored by them all, as he was by his wife, children, grandchildren and great-grandchildren. Beryl treasures the many wonderful letters that she received when he died. All of which speak of a man of outstanding integrity. He left a legacy of memories, of his love, his honesty, his generosity and his loyalty.

Painter family of Hill End Villas

Pamela Painter (now Mrs Sims) writes,

Employment at Hill End with Mr and Mrs Gilbert S. James brought young Minnie Hardwell of Bristol, and Andrew Painter of Kingsdown, Box, together around 1930. Minnie was the family's nursery maid, and Andrew was stable boy at that time. When the children went to boarding school, their services were no longer needed so they took work near Bath, married in 1934, and shared Andrew's family's cottage where I was born in 1935. When I was two years old, Mr James asked Andy to return to his staff with the incentive of a house for the small family – number 1 Hill End Villas.

Andrew, Minnie and Pam at their front door

War started in 1939, and Andy was called up, first serving with the Royal Artillery, then BAOR until he was demobbed in 1946. He then returned to his position of groom at Hill End.

Pam went to the Infants and Girls School in Station Road where her con-

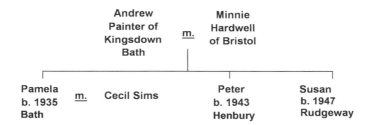

Pam, heading for the tunnel

temporaries included Betty Woodsford and Beryl Love. Robin Broad lived nearby. She spent hours at Ison (Piddley) Hill with Beardsmores, Thomases, Coxes, and also at the 'house in the wall' with the White children. The façade of the house was part of a long high wall running down to the Hamlet. Blaise grounds and woods were their play areas with no need to fear for their safety then.

Pam has a few vivid memories of the war years,

When Dad was away in the army, and the raids were full-blast, our nights were spent in the tunnel which runs between Blaise Hamlet and the Mansion. It was so damp we had to take our bedding to and fro in sack trucks made by Dad during time off on leave. But I thought it was all great fun being there with half the village! We had some good old sing-songs, and a van from Fry's dispensed a nightcap of cocoa.

I also remember leaning over Hallen Road railway bridge watching the bombed oil-storage tanks blazing for days at Avonmouth. And, worst of all, a large water tank in the field next to Hill End Villas took a direct hit one night blasting the poor herd of cows there with shrapnel. Mum cried and cried watching the dead and injured animals being dragged into trucks. Mum remembers one cow with her side torn open looking up at her with pitiful eyes as if to say 'Please help me'.

In 1943, in the middle of the war, my brother Peter was born, delivered by Nurse Beech who lived in the Schoolhouse in Station Road.

As the bombing eased off, we, Mum, brother in pram and me – frequently walked the four miles or so to Severn Beach, a wonderful place in my eyes! At least there was a beach there then. My tired legs were

Miss Vowles' dancing class

spurred on the journey home by trailing a whirly-bird on string, and we sometimes bought juicy Morgan Sweet apples from farms en route.

For Pam, another highlight in the restrictions of war time was dancing class. She danced with the Betty Vowles School of Dancing at Westbury on Trym (a shilling for soft shoe, sixpence for tap). She loved taking part in displays at Canford Park and the Victoria Rooms, especially being allowed to wear her stage make-up home on the bus! Special effort was put into one such display to celebrate the end of the war.

Ingenious mothers made up the costumes, dyeing butter-muslin red, white and blue, and trimmed with braid in these colours. My brother Peter aged three had a habit of throwing everything he could find, including the dance costumes, into the water butt alongside the back door, resulting in purple butter muslin! Our resourceful mother hastened to Mrs Brown's shop in the village street, and saved the day with gauze and coloured inks!

Shortly after the war, the James family moved to Heneage Court in Falfield. In the big freeze of 1947 the Painter family moved to Rudgeway, where their youngest child, Susan was born. This enabled Andy to continue his service with the James family, eventually moving to and managing Heneage Farm for the rest of his working life.

During the summers, Pam cycled from Rudgeway to work at Joe Stevens' Tea Room in Henbury where she was paid 'according to trade', so when it rained she got little return for her wet ride. 'But', she says, 'Mr Stevens was a gentleman, and I was well paid if we were busy. I remember the Miss Perrets and their flowers, small ones arranged attractively in boxes of moss.'

Scott Family of 2, Hill End Villas
Pam Sims stays in touch with Joyce Mossman who was born Joyce Scott. Pam writes, 'Joyce's father was chauffeur to the Jameses, and like the Painters lived at Hill End Villas. We two girls grew up as close neighbours and friends. In the war, Joyce joined the WRNS, and met and married a New Zealand sailor. Joyce and her husband have lived in New Zealand for many years now.'

Cliffords of Westmoreland Cottage
'William Clifford was Head Gardener to Major Sampson Way, and his wife Kate would help out in the Major's kitchen when there were weekend guests.' So writes Mrs Ruby Clifford.

William and Kate had four children, three boys and a girl. When the eldest William George Mervyn was fifteen years old, the family moved to one of the Major's tied houses, Westmoreland Cottage in Crow Lane, opposite Westmoreland Farmhouse. They remained there for about 10 years, before moving to a bungalow nearer to the centre of the village, known as 'Applegarth.' This suited them well, for Kate, a regular churchgoer, was much nearer to St Mary's; and for William, a bell-ringer, one of that gallant band who sounded the 'call to prayer' far and wide for those who had ears to hear! Those 'ringers' also celebrated the solemnity and joy of the young couples of the Parish, arriving for their great day – their

Wedding. There was yet another happy result of the move, for William's 'port of call' on Saturday evenings was the Porter Stores.

In 1939 just before they moved to Applegarth, their eldest son Mervyn was married to Ruby Morse from Westbury Park. The young people set up house in Cotham, later moving to Clifton, near the suspension bridge remaining there for forty years. By then, their second son Stanley had left school (in 1934), and went to work for the Major for six years before joining the Army. Hilda eventually emigrated to Australia, and Ronald was still a schoolboy.

William George Mervyn was employed by Bristol City as a bus conductor from 1939 until retirement, except for the war years when he served with the Sussex Regiment in North Africa. Mervyn died in 1988, but his wife Ruby says that he enjoyed good friendships as a boy in Henbury especially with the Rugman family and Charlie who lived near Blaise.

Ruby was herself brought up in Westbury Park with Durdham Down as her playground. She attended Westbury Park Primary School and then Bishop Road School. She was just two years out of school when she met Mervyn. They married when she was nineteen.

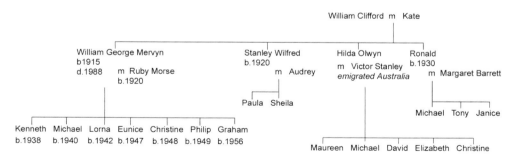

Bill Clifford (right) on a 1930s Bell Ringers' outing

Ruby talked about her father and her father-in-law,

> They both served in the Great War, Mervyn's father, a gardener from
> Tetbury served as a cook, and my Dad served in the Veterinary Corps
> caring for the horses. After the war they returned to gardening, my
> father becoming gardener to the School for the Blind in Henleaze.
> When Mervyn and I were getting married, his father tried to breed a
> black or dark red carnation for the wedding bouquet, but it wasn't
> ready in time. When my first baby was born, he brought peaches and
> black grapes from the Major's greenhouses. The family always used to
> refer to the Major as 'Squire'.

Mervyn and Ruby had seven children, all of whom started their schooling
at Christchurch Primary School in Clifton. The eldest two proceeded to
Portway School, and the rest to Ashton Park School.

Stanley Clifford
Stanley attended Henbury Boys School whose Head Master at that time
was Mr Denis Smart. Other teachers Stanley remembers were Mr Dai
Davis, Miss Brown, Miss Capewell. He remembers the ceremony of 'clipping the church', Mr Lloyd was vicar then. Stanley writes down the prayer

Kate Clifford: war work at Filton

at the end of lessons every day:

> Lord, keep us safe this night,
> Secure from all our fears.
> May angels guard us while we sleep
> Till morning light appears.

In reminiscent mood, Stanley continues,

> Henbury Church bells on Sunday evenings
> [rang out] across sunlit meadows.

Some of his boyhood pursuits were,

playing football on recreation ground in Station Road near cottages called 'Botany Bay' with Albert Hodges, Sid Shepherd. We visited the Carlton Cinema twice a week at 9d, entrance. In the evenings, we listened to the radio. I helped Dad in his allotment and in the garden. We

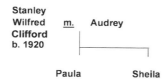

helped on Westmoreland Farm, cleaning fowl house, and unchaining cows after milking. (Miss Doll Smith had a tennis court). At one time, I delivered papers for Mrs Brown, general store in the village street, whose son was an England Rugby player. Then there was the Henbury Flower Show. Once, I entered a map of England, and mis-spelt the River Severn, and was ordered to keep away from the Show!

I remember Henbury Golf Club – through the tunnel field and Blaise Castle land. Pro. Jack Branch had a son Leslie. He and I earned coppers finding golf balls for Members; and later on, caddied for 1/6 per round.

Two woodsmen came down once a year to clip the two rows of yew trees, and to supply logs of wood from Berwick Woods owned by Major Sampson Way. My family, by the way, used to refer to the Major as 'Squire'. He had a kitchen garden, walled in grapes, peaches.

Other things that I call to mind are that Mr Townsend was Landlord of the Porter Stores, Woodbine 'cigs' were 2d a packet of five, Bitter was 4d per pint. At weekends, Walls ice-cream was sold from a box on a tricycle.

Two chauffeurs I remember were Mr Powesland who worked for Dr Wills, of The Old Rectory, and Sid Shepherd who was chauffer to the Major.

When I came back from the War, the family had moved to Keynsham.

Ronald Clifford

William and Kate's youngest child, Ronald was nine years old at the outbreak of World War II. He attended Henbury Boys School in the Close, opposite his house. He had many friends in the village. Peter Baguley living almost next door at sexton's cottage and Peter Powesland. Together they roamed the Blaise Castle woods, and got up to mischief, sometimes being the bane of their neighbours, especially the Miss Perretts whose garden backed onto the Cliffords' garden. Ronnie says,

On one occasion a friend and I pulled up beansticks that had just been carefully placed to support growing runner beans. The temptation was too great as we could reach the sticks from the communal wall. Then

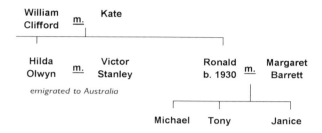

```
        William        Kate
        Clifford   m.
        ┌───────────────┴──────────────────────────┐
     Hilda         Victor           Ronald     Margaret
     Olwyn    m.   Stanley          b. 1930  m. Barrett
       emigrated to Australia
                                   ┌──────┼──────────┐
                              Michael   Tony      Janice
```

I was a choirboy! I remember Mr Ubank standing behind the boys in the choirmen's stall would prod our backs as a warning against any brewing mischief. Mrs Ubank gave a great deal of time to cleaning brass, arranging flowers and other good works. The church and school were the focus of village life. Everyone knew everyone, and there was a great sense of community.

On leaving school at fourteen, Ron went to help his father on the market garden he kept on the field next to the Hamlet and opposite Blaise Castle gates. The family later moved to a house in Hallen, 'The Barton', opposite the 'King Billy'. For three or four years, Ronnie worked as Fireman with G. W. R. Railway until diesel engines took over from steam. In those days he used to cycle from Hallen to Temple Meads Station every day. He did his National Service at Catterick Camp 1948 to 1950. After that and for the rest of his working life, he was a theatre porter at Southmead Hospital in Bristol.

In 1953, he married Margaret Barrett, and they have three children, Michael, Tony and Janice. Ronald is now a venerable grandfather but still very young at heart.

He relates a few anecdotes from his youth, obviously enjoying his memories of an extremely happy childhood.

When I was very young, we lived at Westmoreland Cottage opposite Westmoreland Farmhouse. In front of the farmhouse garden wall was an area of grass. I used to cross the lane and go and pick daisies there. Ray's Aunt Doll used to come out and talk to me, and she taught me how to make daisy chains. Ray himself would sometimes come out with a hosepipe, waggle it about and frighten me, saying it was a snake! He only had to say 'I'm going to get the snake out' and I would become alarmed. Aunt Doll sometimes gave me strawberries and cream to eat in the courtyard by the bakery.

I recall that Dr Wills of the Old Rectory ran Bible classes for the village mothers, and Miss Aldridge of Chesterfield (Chest-of-Drawers) House also ran Bible classes. It was a tight-knit community, and all joined in.

When I was five or six years old, I remember sitting on the green by the ford, and watching the first double-decker bus go by. In large printed letters on the side was SWAN VESTA. It did a circular route, Westbury on Trym, Brentry, Henbury, Hallen. The bus doing the opposite run had MICKLEBURGH PIANOS written along it.

We played tennis on the courts behind the Georgian cottages, and we played on the golf course, but not golf, rather adventures and rough and tumble. In summer, there were many visitors to Blaise Castle Estate. Coaches would line up in Church Lane outside our house to bring in and out people from all over Bristol. The Stevens family did a great trade in their small café next to the Post Office.

After the Major's death, my father went out to Keynsham to start up a market gardening business. And so the Clifford family ceased to be part of the once rural community of Henbury.

4
Two farming families
Hignell and Biggs (an extended family)

Westmoreland, Norton and The Elms were the three commercial farms in Henbury before the Second World War. The McEwen Smiths had arrived in the village in the nineteenth century, the Hignells and Biggs arrived in the early twentieth century. All had a long history in farming. In this chapter, a little of the ancestry of the Hignells and Biggs will be looked at, as well as a glimpse into their everyday life.

The Hignell Family
The family traces its ancestry to at least mid-eighteenth century and to Joseph Hignell who married Elizabeth Meare in 1788. Although Joseph originated in Elberton, he lived in the Thornbury area of Gloucestershire. He was a farmer, and this profession was followed down the generations. Joseph and Elizabeth had a number of children, but George, the eldest is of special interest to this study because the Henbury Hignells descend from him and his wife in two main branches.

George (Hignell I)
George married Hannah Smith, and their two elder sons were George and Thomas – later to head the two Henbury Hignell families.

George (Hignell II)
This George married Sarah Williams, and their eldest son was George Philip Albert:

George (Hignell III)
George Philip Albert married Henrietta Tedder from Westbury on Trym. Their son was Henry George Hignell.

George and Sarah farmed at Lawrence Weston. Their son George Philip Albert was mainly a cattle-broker, but also kept a small herd of cows. Ray McEwen Smith remembered that George kept his Guernsey cows on Blaise Castle land rented from the Harford Estate, and then the City

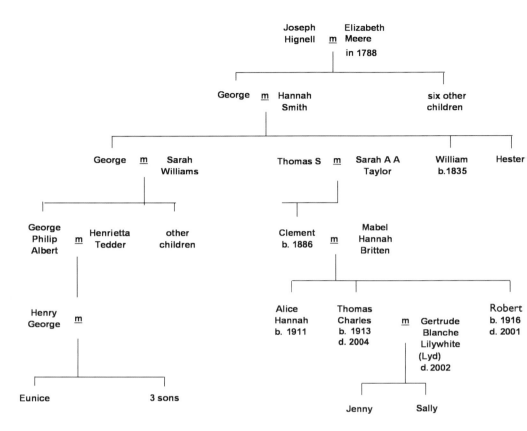

Council. When Ray was about ten years old, he used to go with George in his old horse and cart out to milk the cows in the field. Sometimes it was difficult to get the cows to stand still in the open fields to be milked. When Ray grew up and became a farmer, George, who had been his grandfather's friend became his friend and adviser.

Henry George

George III's son Henry George as a very young man started a milk round, carrying can and ladle on the handlebars of his pushbike. In course of time, Henry George (known as Harry) who lived in a cottage (which is still there) in Passage Road with his wife built up a profitable business bottling milk in a shed by his house. Later, the family established a thriving small store in Crow Lane.

Thomas Hignell

Thomas, son of George I and brother of George II married Sarah Taylor, and they farmed at Hallen. Clement, born 1886 was brought up as an only child, unusual in those days.

Clement Hignell

Clement married Hannah Britten whose father farmed Miners Farm in Hallen. They had three children, Alice Hannah, Thomas Charles and Robert. For the first five years of their marriage, Clement and Hannah rented a farm in Lawrence Weston. Then in 1917 Clement took over the tenancy of Norton Farm in Henbury where they remained for the rest of their working lives.

Thomas Hignell (known to all as Tom)

Tom says that one of his earliest memories was in 1917 when he was four years old. He and his mother, and Bob (in pushchair), looked over Henbury Station from the bridge, and saw the Royal train when King George V was travelling to Avonmouth. It had stopped there for the night, and a circle of soldiers was positioned in the fields to guard the train and its occupant. The local Girls School gathered on the platform to greet the King.

Tom grew up very happily at Norton Farm with his sister and brother. He enjoyed helping on the farm and following many country pursuits. He attended school at Redland Hill House, but as he approached his teens, his father Clem, who suffered severely from rheumatism, was becoming increasingly disabled. Tom left school at thirteen and took over much of the heavy work from his father. His brother Bob followed suit a few years later.

But it wasn't all work and no play! In his later teens, Tom started to go about with a group of friends, both boys and girls. He had always been close to his cousin Elaine, and these two formed the core of the group. They went to the cinema (the Carlton in Westbury on Trym) and to dances in the village halls of Westbury, Stoke Bishop, Henbury and Hallen. But these were not the only leisure pursuits of the young Hignells. They were all, parents and children alike, involved in the worship and social life of their village parish church. Then there were agricultural shows and competitions and co-operative projects with other local farmers. They knew

Edna Cullimore with Blossom

their close neighbours at Botany Bay and other cottages. They employed labour forces as well as casual workers and schoolchildren. The boys walked, rode bicycles and drove horse-drawn carts.

They moved stock about, sometimes to and from market, and sometimes to the slaughter house, on one occasion with near-disaster. Tom relates:

> A farm labourer and I were taking three fat steers to Ellings slaughter-house in Westbury on Trym when one steer escaped across the golf course into the wood. It fell over the cliff onto the thatched roof of Mrs Pearce's kitchen where a ham was simmering in the boiler. Mrs Pearce must have been a survivor for she experienced yet another similar dis-aster later. It was again one of my animals that caused havoc in Mrs Pearce's house, the second lodge of Blaise from the hill-top gate. Blossom had been loaned to a council workman who was removing rubbish near the lodge where the narrow lane to the golf course branches off. The labourer took the horse and cart to the top of the lane, and turned it, facing downhill. Not having brakes, he wedged the front wheel with a stone. Blossom strained over the stone, charged for-ward, missed the bend, and went straight on through the cottage win-dow, ending up with its two front legs on the sofa! A crowbar burst the door open in order to undo the harness and free the horse. Fortunately Mrs Pearce was away from home at that time-but what a homecoming! She was an amazing woman for she seemed to hold no rancour.

Tom and his friend Ben Thurston offered Mrs Pearce a lift home every Sunday from evening service to which she regularly walked. Tom still remembers the slice of home-made cake she invariably rewarded them with. Tom then remembered that Ben in later days as a Charlton farmer was very badly affected when Charlton village was bulldozed in order to extend Filton runway for the Bristol Brabazon.

Tom grew to adulthood, and after a lapse of years met up again with one of his group of youthful friends. Tom remembers:

> She was Elaine's special friend, Gertrude Blanche Lilywhite, a farmer's daughter. Blanche, Elaine and a third friend who were apprentice hairdressers together gave each other nicknames. Blanche was nicknamed 'Lyd', and it stuck to her all her life.

Tom and Lyd

Tom proposed to Lyd on a long day trip to London, his first foray into the capital, and in 1944 they were married. Then Clement and Tom divided the farmhouse between them, and became joint tenants of Major Sampson Way's. This proved a good arrangement because the house was large enough for the two families, and Tom and Bob could still work as a team with their father. Eventually Bob married, and rented his own farm beyond Westbury.

A few years later, a compulsory purchase order robbed them of half their joint tenancy, but they were able to repurchase the remainder from the remnant of the Major's Estate. Clement died shortly after this, and Tom bought his father's share of the farm from the rest of the family.

When their historic and beautiful farmstead was demolished by the Council for new housing development, Tom and Lyd moved to North Hill Cottage where they brought up their two daughters, Jenny and Sally. When their daughters were launched into the world, and into marriage, and as Tom and Lyd grew old, they retired to a bungalow in Charlton Lane. Later still, they moved to a Retirement Home where Lyd could receive the nursing care that she needed. After her death, Tom remained at Almondsbury, still ready to tell stories of his farming life, until his death in Autumn 2004.

I think it is fitting to add a note about his accident-prone horse 'Blossom'. Mr Lionel Kite wrote a note about his wife Edna Cullimore, who lived as a child at Botany Bay Cottages:

> Edna grew up in Henbury. In the early fifties, she worked for Tom Hignell at Norton Farm. It was here that I first met her. I have a picture of Edna with Blossom that I thought you might like to use in the chapter about Tom Hignell. I am sadly now a widower, and I remember those farming days with great pleasure.

Biggs dynasty: Foxley to Henbury, an extended family

Roy Pearce, Victor Goodfield and Robert Biggs find a common ancestor in James Biggs:

Family members agree that Foxley and Norton are the Wiltshire villages from where their ancestors originated. However, further evidence indicates an ancestor, one Richard Biggs who was born in Marshfield in 1624, and whose wife was named Annie. They are followed by James born in 1690 in Hawkesbury, and his wife, Mary. Then there is Robert, christened in 1716, also at Hawkesbury, and his wife, Hannah. Finally there is James Biggs who was christened in 1741 at Didmarton.

James Biggs and his wife Mary had at least seven children, the youngest of whom was John, born 1790. John married Ann Goodman and they had two daughters and two sons born at Norton in Wiltshire. The two boys William and John married two sisters from Foxley, Harriet and Margaret Boucher. It is from these two couples that the Biggs from Henbury and Hallen are descended. It would appear that Foxley, and Red House Farm in Coombe Dingle Bristol, are strong in the memories of some of them – and indeed provide a common link between them. They are proud to come of farming stock who specialized in dairy farming.

Red House Farm

John and Margaret (ancestors of Robert Biggs and Victor Goodfield)
John and his family are known to have lived within the Parsonage at Foxley 1860-1871 when John worked at Foxley Farm. Later, he went to live and work at Red House Farm in the Parish of Westbury on Trym. Of the three daughters and three sons born to John and Margaret, William and Annie became the ancestors of the families who settled in Henbury and Hallen. George Henry, the youngest son continued with his family to farm at Red House Farm, Coldharbour and Redland Green Farms at different times. Details of the family tree have been supplied by a husband of one of George Henry's descendants.

Foxley Church

The Census of 1881 shows John at Red House Farm as Farm Bailiff with his sons James and George working as Dairymen (also nephew John). It also shows the eldest son William with his wife Louisa, as 'Farmer of 80 acres' of the same farm.

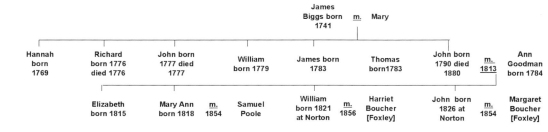

The Elms Dairy Farm in 1906

William and Louisa Biggs

In about 1906, William and Louisa moved to The Elms Farm in Henbury with their children. At William's death in 1911, his twenty four year old son Robert Stanley took over The Elms, now a dairy farm and, following the success of his father, built up a herd of Guernsey cattle, an up-to-date dairy and a team of roundsmen to transport the produce to customers in their homes. In time, R. S. Biggs' son Robert took over the farm until, in the 1970s he moved his herd westward into Somerset, as Henbury developed from a small village to a suburb.

Annie Biggs

She was John and Margaret's eldest daughter. In 1878 she married John Goodfield from Foxley. They had three daughters, Elizabeth, Lilian and Margaret, and four sons, Frank, Albert, William and George. In World War I, George joined the Canadian Army.

His son Victor says,

> My father returned to Henbury, married, and went to work for a coal merchant. My mother was Daisy Laura Joyner. I had a sister who was the oldest, then two brothers before I was born in 1926. I well remem-

The Biggs Family

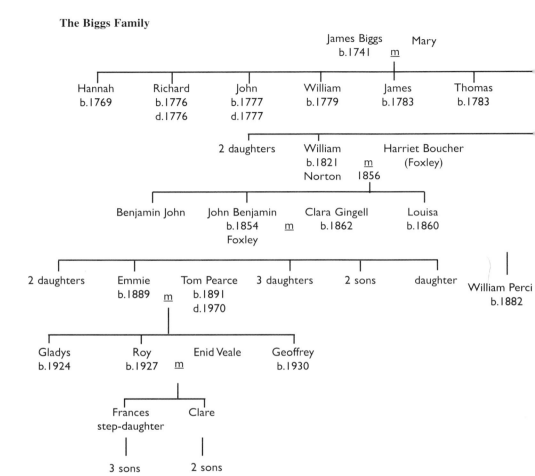

James Biggs
b.1741   <u>m</u>   Mary

Hannah	Richard	John	William	James	Thomas
b.1769	b.1776	b.1777	b.1779	b.1783	b.1783
	d.1776	d.1777			

2 daughters   William   Harriet Boucher
          b.1821   <u>m</u>   (Foxley)
          Norton   1856

Benjamin John   John Benjamin   Clara Gingell   Louisa
             b.1854   <u>m</u>   b.1862   b.1860
             Foxley

2 daughters   Emmie   Tom Pearce   3 daughters   2 sons   daughter
          b.1889   b.1891   William Perci
               <u>m</u>   d.1970   b.1882

Gladys   Roy   Enid Veale   Geoffrey
b.1924   b.1927   <u>m</u>   b.1930

Frances   Clare
step-daughter

3 sons   2 sons

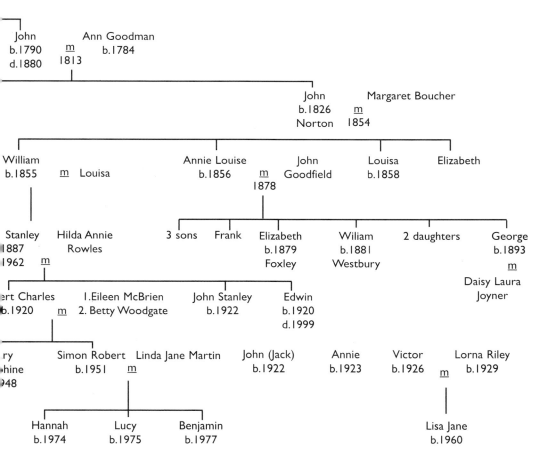

John
b.1790   m   Ann Goodman
d.1880   1813   b.1784

John
b.1826   m   Margaret Boucher
Norton   1854

William   Annie Louise   John   Louisa   Elizabeth
b.1855   m Louisa   b.1856   m Goodfield   b.1858
                          1878

Stanley   Hilda Annie   3 sons   Frank   Elizabeth   Wiliam   2 daughters   George
1887   Rowles   b.1879   b.1881   b.1893
1962   m   Foxley   Westbury   m
                                                                      Daisy Laura
                                                                       Joyner

ert Charles   1.Eileen McBrien   John Stanley   Edwin
b.1920   m   2. Betty Woodgate   b.1922   b.1920
                                              d.1999

ry   Simon Robert   Linda Jane Martin   John (Jack)   Annie   Victor   Lorna Riley
hine   b.1951   m   b.1922   b.1923   b.1926   m   b.1929
948
                                                                      Lisa Jane
Hannah   Lucy   Benjamin   b.1960
b.1974   b.1975   b.1977

79

The tree of William and Louisa Biggs

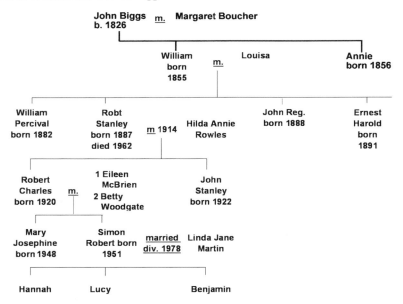

ber our cottages set among fields and fronting on to Station Road that carried only horses pulling coal carts and carriages, and people walking to the Station to catch the train to work at Avonmouth. I remember the single water pump serving all the cottages, the long front gardens, the friendly neighbours. Next door were the Woodsfords. My sister Annie used to play with their little girl, Betty. There was Harold Godfrey, a much bigger boy than me, Arthur Cox and his brother, and so many others. It was a pleasant community.

William & Harriet Biggs (ancestor of Roy Pearce)

William, elder son of John and Ann, and brother to John married Harriet Boucher who was sister to John's wife Margaret. Their first baby, Benjamin John died. When their second son was born in 1858 they named him John Benjamin. Two years later, they had a daughter Louise. Their grandson Roy Pearce has always believed that his grandfather John Benjamin was orphaned in early life. The lack of children after Louise's birth in days when large families were the custom might suggest that the mother died young.

The Biggs Family tree – Roy Pearce's branch

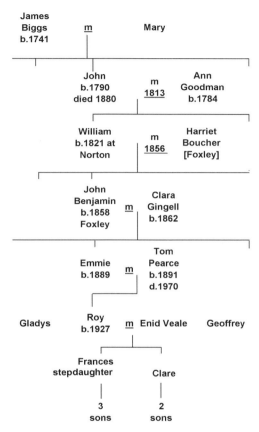

But evidence shows that the father lived until the children were grown up because William's signature is on his son John's marriage certificate. However, Roy says that from about twelve years of age, John lived with his uncle John at Red House Farm.

In the census of 1881, John at the age of twenty-two was working at Red House Farm as Dairyman, and his sister Louise was working as a servant elsewhere. On his marriage to Clara Gingell in 1884 the couple went to live in Clifton. Some time after this John was working as carter for the Corn Merchant on High Street in Westbury on Trym. He lived with his wife in one of the cottages behind Drew's Stores, and kept his horse in the

John Benjamin and Clara brought up their nine children in this cottage in Hallen. It was later demolished to build the motorway bridge

Stables that later became Pratts' Garage.

The cottage was small so they soon moved to a house in Hallen called Cumberland Cottages where John Benjamin and his wife Clara brought up their nine children, seven girls and two boys. Later still they moved to Cambridge Crescent in Westbury, into some older cottages on the bend of the road from where their eldest daughter was married. Eventually all the girls went into service, and John and Clara moved to 3, College Road in Westbury.

Their third daughter Emily (Emmie) married Thomas Pearce, and they first set up house in Bishopston. When Roy was twelve months old, they went back to Westbury to number 3 Church Road. These cottages were later demolished but are thought to have been part of the building next door which was The White Horse Inn. Roy remembers that their cottages shared cellars and courtyard with the Inn, and all the houses had interconnecting doors. Roy lived there happily with his elder sister Gladys and a younger brother Geoffrey.

Roy attended Westbury Church School that held only Infants and Junior classes. So at eleven years old Roy was sent to Henbury Boys School to which he cycled. (He left his bike in the Gunns' coach house while he was at school.) He believes the reason for the choice of Henbury was family tradition. His mother and her sisters and brothers had all gone to school in Henbury, and later, his younger brother Geoffrey also went there. His schoolmates were his friends, and he played football with the Hallen and Henbury United. As he left school at the age of fourteen, their cottages were condemned, and the family moved to Sea Mills.

Roy, a Coronation photograph

During the war, when there were air raids, the children went out of school to shelter in the cellars of Blaise Castle House. The girls came from Station Road via the tunnel under Kings Weston Road and across the lawn to the house.

Roy remembers the Flower Show, and that horse-drawn carts came to it from far and wide, driving through Westbury, the horses would be watered there at the horse trough that was in front of the present Post Office. He remembers enjoying dances with his school friends at Hallen, and church services at Henbury especially Ash Wednesday and Good Friday when they had the day off school.

When Roy left school, he joined the Railway in whose employ he remained until retirement. He married Enid Veale. They have one daughter Clare who is now married with two boys, and Roy's stepdaughter

Frances who has three sons. Roy is a cheerful man with many interests, an important one of which is researching his family origins. He looks back on his schooldays with pleasure.

Roy has another connection with Henbury, for his mother's youngest sister Violet married Albert Woodsford of Botany Bay Cottages who was gardener to Mr Gunn, and others locally, such as the owners of Henbury Court.

5

Small neighbourhoods and communities

Botany Bay: Godfrey, Goodfield and Cox
Ison Hill: Steer and Lane

In this chapter we look at small neighbourhoods or communities of families, some of whom were employed in the village, others were self-employed or acting as business agents; in Botany Bay the Godfrey family, Goodfields and Coxes; and in Ison Hill, the Steer family. Note: the third community was Blaise Hamlet, and this has been described by the Warburton Family of Henbury Post Office.

Ken Lane of The King William in Hallen is here regarded as a close neighbour and friend of Henbury.

Godfrey Family of 4 Botany Bay Cottages, Station Road

Harold Godfrey writes:

> My father Frederick Godfrey from Coombe Dingle, served with the Machine Gun Corps in the 1914-18 Great War. He married my mother Emily Ada Sparks, a Somerset girl. Fred first worked as a coachman in Sneyd Park where I was born. Later, he became an insurance agent, and we went to live in Henbury, at Botany Bay Cottages.

Harold and his sister Marion grew up in these rural surroundings, and enjoyed a very happy childhood. Lack of amenities such as electricity, gas and mains water meant that they had to cook and heat water on a coal-fired range, use oil lamps for lighting (large ones downstairs and small ones to take up to the bedrooms), and every drop of water had to be carried from the communal pump outside number six. Their house was double-fronted, and a long path from the gate led to the front door between two strips of garden used to grow vegetables. Coal had to be carried this way and through the house to a coal house at the back. All the rooms except the back bedroom had fireplaces, but there was no bathroom or lavatory in the house. That small room was outside, in the back yard next to the wash-house.

At Christmas, the puddings were cooked in the wash-house boiler. All

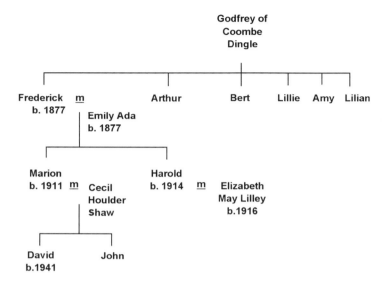

year round, the weekly bath was taken in a zinc bath by the boiler, as well as the weekly wash (laundry).

Harold recalls those far-off days,

> In my childhood, Henbury, not much bigger than a hamlet, was very rural. The air was clean and fresh, and the only transport passing our houses were the coal carts pulled by large horses from Station Yard, and the horse-drawn carriages visiting Henbury Court through a gate opposite to our cottages.

> Among our neighbours we had plenty of friends, Price, Woodsford, Greenfield, Cox and Cullimore families. Many of these remained in their houses for years, providing happy stability for the children. My best friend was Henry Price who lived with his family at number 8. Henry won an exam to go to Rendcombe College. He then went to Elder and Fyffes and got his Master's Certificate. But he couldn't get a job, so joined the River Police finishing as Inspector at Trinity Road.

> Dad was an Insurance Agent, and mother looked after the housekeeping. My sister Marion and I started school at the Infants Class at the Henbury Girls School a little further down Station Road. When I was seven, I moved to the Boys School in Church Lane (now the Village

Hall). Marion and her friends moved from the Infants Class to the Girls Class in the Station Road building. We both left school at the age of fourteen.

Harold says he spent a very happy childhood with plenty of interesting things to do. They roamed the countryside walking and biking, helped on the farms and gardens. There were special days also. Opposite Botany Bay and to the east of Henbury Court were double gates leading to the Hotel and a field where the annual Hallen Horse Show was held. (At an earlier time, it had been held on Sampson Way's field where the Flower Show was once held) A short walk across the road, and the Godfrey children enjoyed a lovely day out. Then there was the Hallen and Henbury Flower Show held behind the ford on Sampson Way fields. They also enjoyed numerous Sunday School Outings, and Harold went to Choir Outings.

Harold remembers,

> When I was seven I moved to the Boys School – also Henry Price took me to join the choir. I was read out by Canon Way in 1928, and went as Server, but I had to give it up when I had to work some Sunday mornings. I was made Sidesman in 1980 and I acted as Verger at weddings and funerals. Also I opened the church at 8 am, and continued verger's duty until I left the Bristol area in 2002.

As a small child he and Marion and their friends played together on Station Road (quite safe then!). As he grew older, he took up cycling and gardening, but his favourite pastime was football which he played at school on the Rec in their ordinary clothes. He and his friends were very keen, and founded the Henbury Robins, a group of schoolboys who were befriended by Mrs Gunn of Henbury House who let them take baths in her house after matches, provided them with football shirts and transport to 'away' matches. Home matches were held on the Arthur Baker Memorial Ground (the Rec). The whole family attended Services at St Mary's church and most of the social functions there also. Harold was a member of the Communicants Guild as well as the choir.

When Harold left school at fourteen, he went to work at the flour mill in Avonmouth. The flour adversely affected his health so he went to work on

Harold in uniform

the buses, first as a conductor, then as a driver – a job he continued for forty-six years until retirement.

Harold grew up, and married Elizabeth May Lilley from Avonmouth. She worked in a drapers' shop in Gloucester Road, and he would wait for her every morning. He took his new wife to live with his parents at Botany Bay. Harold recalls their great holidays at that time:

We had a tandem and spent holidays touring Devon, Cornwall, North and South Wales. In 1962 I bought a Morris 1000 to take my mother and older folks about.

When it was decided to demolish the Botany Bay Cottages, Betty and Harold in 1951 moved to a one bedroom flat in Satchfield Crescent, and in 1956 they moved to Westbury Park. They still attended St Mary's Henbury, and for many years, Harold lovingly tended the roses in the churchyard.

Harold's parents moved, in about 1952, to one of the first block of flats to be built in Station Road. His sister Marion married Cecil Houldershaw, and they have two sons.

Victor Goodfield and his family: Botany Bay Cottages
George Goodfield joined the Canadian Army in the First World War. After the war he returned to Henbury. There he married Daisy Laura Joyner and went to work for a coal merchant.

George and Daisy had four children, Edwin, Annie, Victor and John (Jack). They lived at number 1 Botany Bay Cottages, and Daisy's family, the Joyners lived at the last house in the row, near to Norton Farm.

Victor Goodfield recalls:

> When I was very small, my father with a colleague, Mr Brown set up a coal merchant company in the Station Yard in Henbury, Brown and Goodfield. Coal was used extensively both commercially and domestically, so the new service while benefiting the Company gave valuable service to the village. We lived at our Botany Bay cottage until 1935 with very minor improvements to the facilities. Then we moved to the one-time Inn, the old Lamb and Flag. Dad rented it from Silvey's, another coal merchant. My brother was Silvey's gardener.

> In our country village it was quiet and peaceful. we all went to St Mary's Church for Services and most of our social life. I joined Scouts, and we played cricket on the 'Rec'. My friends and I joined the Church Choir, and I carried the Cross in processions. We were all great cyclists, visiting places such as Chepstow and Symonds Yat, and from Henbury to Tintern Abbey. It should be remembered that almost the only traffic was horse-drawn. Harold Godfrey once cycled to Birmingham!

> We played tennis at Canford Park and at Henbury Hill House (Didsbury College). We joined the farmers in hay-making. I had many friends at Henbury Boys School, especially Bob Tucker, and friends among our close neighbours. The Woodsfords lived next door, and my sister Annie played with Betty Woodsford. I knew Harold Godfrey, but he was a little older than me. Arthur Cox was a friend.

> I started school at the Infants Class in Station Road (Girls and Infants) before moving to Henbury Boys in Church Close. After leaving school, I spent three months assisting the Schoolmaster; then I joined the Bristol Aeroplane Company where I worked in the Mailing Department.

> As I grew up we attended dances at Village Halls as well as other places. A favourite venue was Brentry House Colony for the mentally handicapped. They gave good dances. The young residents were from wealthy families, and everything was of high quality. (Some residents worked for my father.)

> Then I met Lorna Bailey who lived at Brentry Lodge Cottages, and not

The Goodfield Family tree

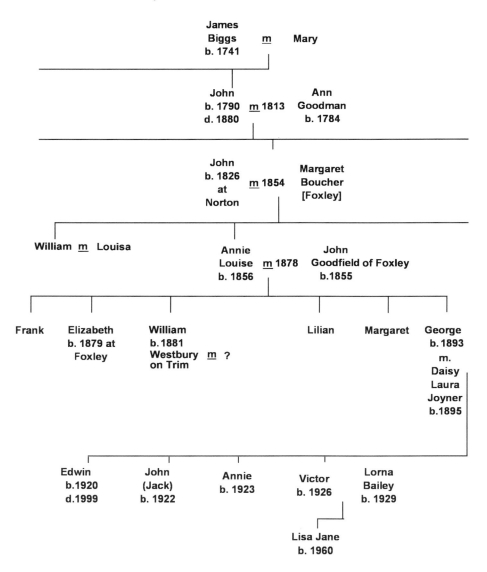

James Biggs b. 1741 **m** Mary

John b. 1790 d. 1880 **m** 1813 Ann Goodman b. 1784

John b. 1826 at Norton **m** 1854 Margaret Boucher [Foxley]

William **m** Louisa

Annie Louise b. 1856 **m** 1878 John Goodfield of Foxley b.1855

Frank

Elizabeth b. 1879 at Foxley

William b.1881 Westbury on Trim **m** ?

Lilian

Margaret

George b. 1893 m. Daisy Laura Joyner b.1895

Edwin b.1920 d.1999

John (Jack) b. 1922

Annie b. 1923

Victor b. 1926

Lorna Bailey b. 1929

Lisa Jane b. 1960

long after, we married.

Lorna remembers,

> One of our pastimes was a club I formed with my friend Joy Hodges
> (Nurseryman Hodges' daughter), and ten others. We played table-ten-
> nis, went for long walks, for instance from Brentry to the Suspension
> Bridge, along the river bank to Pill, and back across the ferry to Sea
> Mills, and then home. Victor was also a member, and we called it the
> '21 Club'. On leaving school, I worked at Dingles Department Store,
> and later at the Hignells' Dairy Shop opposite my family home.

Lorna and Victor married, and their daughter Lisa Jane was born in 1960.

Cox Family of 8 Botany Bay Cottage
(not the same Cox family who were friends of Victor & Harold)

In 1932 William Henry Cox married Agnes Louise Castell, and they went
to live at number 8 Botany Bay Cottages. One of their children remembers
that her grandmother was Welsh (with a temper!)

William Henry and Agnes Louise Cox had five children, two girls and
three boys. Their second child and elder girl, Shirley says that after starting school at the Infants Class in Station Road, she spent many years in
and out of hospital suffering from rheumatic fever. At fourteen, she attended the Open Air School at Knole, remaining there until she was sixteen.
She was also afflicted with a weak heart and cancerous bone. Looking
back to her childhood, much of which she enjoyed, she regrets that the
extra parental care that she received may have caused deprivation to her
sister and brothers.

Shirley had a number of friends in the Cottages, though she was almost a
generation later than Harold Godfrey and his pals. She remembers the
Cullimores at number fourteen. The three girls, Edna and twins Jean and
Joan, were her playmates, and she has happy memories of those days in
spite of everything. She writes:

> I played with Jean and Joan Cullimore next to their cottage, over the
> wall was a small wood. We had a den there where we used to keep bis-
> cuits and drinks. I can remember us sitting on the wall where we

The Cox Family tree

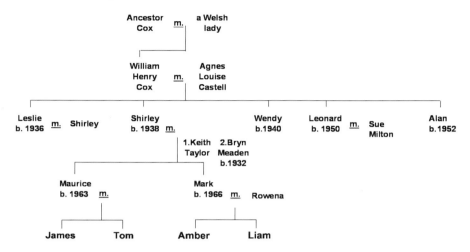

watched the plane, the Brabazon fly over.

My cottage had three rooms upstairs and two rooms downstairs, one had a bay window. I remember we used to put the Christmas tree in the bay, and Dad made the fairy lights run from the accumulator that was normally used for the radio.

At the back of our cottage we had a yard with a toilet that we shared with Mrs Bow. Next to it was a door that went out into the allotments. Up against the wall of our yard on the allotments side, my dad had put a sidecar from a motorbike that we played in. We played all the time in the road – not many cars on the roads then. We used to play a lot over Henbury Court, and in the trenches the soldiers had dug in the wood next to the Court.

There was a long charcoal path up to the back of the school. I remember the school rooms, one long one looked on to the field – In the field were three swings, and one had a longer seat that rocked from front to back. This was next to what we called 'our air-raid shelter', with a cricket pavilion on the other side of the three swings. The school had one small playground with toilet adjoining the bike shed. At the back of the bike shed was another playground and another building. I remember that it had stairs that 'went round' – in a spiral. I remember doing some cooking there. The teachers then were Miss Weekes, Miss Moody, Miss Holden. Another classroom looked out on the nurses' garden. Two District Nurses lived in the house joining the school. We used to go to church with the school, and I remember when we held hands round the church. (clipping the church.)

I walked to Westbury on Saturdays to do the shopping, but came back on the bus. I used to go in a shop to get tea, where the lady, Miss Cook used to give me sweets in a three-corner bag.

Shirley and Wendy

There were two men living next door to us. One man, I think his name was Charlie had a permanently turned head. The other one was called George.

Shirley grew up and married Keith Taylor, which failed. She then married for a second time to Bryn Meaden and had two sons, Maurice and Mark. Mark now has two sons also.

Ison Hill

There was another small community within Henbury. These houses were built about a century later than Botany Bay by Gloucester County Council. Some residents of Botany Bay moved to Ison Hill because there were more up-to-date amenities.

Steer Family of 2 Ison Hill

Bob Steer writes:

> To the best of my knowledge the houses at Ison Hill were built some-time during the late 1920s and consist of six blocks of four terraced houses. The area was still very rural then, and the road saw very little vehicular traffic. At this time one of the few tradesmen that did come

to the area was a milkman. He had a motorcycle with a flat bed side-car, which had a milk churn attached. He would then sound a horn or hooter, and people would come out with jugs or other types of receptacles into which he would decant the required amount of milk. It was at this time that I started attending the Infants' school on Station Road with a view to going to the Boys' school in the village when I reached the age of 7.

At the start of the war it was apparent that the port of Avonmouth would be a prime target for bombing, as it was used for bringing in and storing all the petrol supplies for the West Country. An enormous civil engineering project was then undertaken to remove all the offloaded petrol from the docks, and store it in a safe place away from the area. The site that was chosen was about 6 miles south east of Avonmouth, and situated on the north side of the railway line. This site was about 200 yards from my home, and stretched right up to Berwick woods and went all the way out to Cribbs Causeway. The diggers came and removed huge swathes of earth from the hillside, and then the construction people started assembling and welding enormous steel tanks to contain the petrol. All the joining and inter-joining pipes were then concreted into position, and the soil was piled back over the completed tanks to give the same approximate profile as before. When all the grass etc was finally established, from the air there seemed to be no change in the topography of the area. Each tank held millions of gallons of fuel and each tank could be accessed from a terminal point below Ison Hill on the Hallen side. To a boy of 8 or 9 years old, this was terribly exciting to have a large project such as this on your own doorstep.

During the war a great deal of bombs were aimed at Avonmouth, but the vast majority of the fuel was away from the docks and in the safety of the storage tanks. Sometimes the enemy would drop flares at night to try to find the storage tanks, but they did not succeed as time proved. The only casualty that I can remember was a large water tank that supplied drinking water to the Hallen area. It was a steel structure about the size of a two-storey house. It sustained a direct hit and the next day the surrounding fields were flooded to a depth of 6-7 inches (nice welly-wading depth).

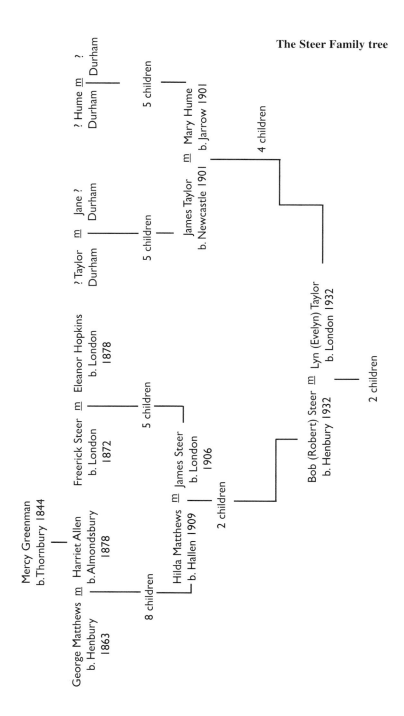

The Steer Family tree

? Hume m ?
Durham | Durham

5 children

James Taylor m Mary Hume
b. Newcastle 1901 b. Jarrow 1901

4 children

? Taylor m Jane ?
Durham | Durham

5 children

Freerick Steer m Eleanor Hopkins
b. London b. London
1872 1878

5 children

Bob (Robert) Steer m Lyn (Evelyn) Taylor
b. Henbury 1932 b. London 1932

2 children

Mercy Greenman
b.Thornbury 1844

George Matthews m Harriet Allen
b. Henbury b. Almondsbury
1863 1878

8 children

Hilda Matthews m James Steer
b. Hallen 1909 b. London
1906

2 children

Jim Steer, wartime Italy

My father was called up into the army (Royal Artillery), where he eventually ended up in North Africa and Italy. At this early age I was put into the position of being the man of the house with a mother and younger brother to look after. Because of rationing and shortages things had to be done to get by. Growing food items was a big priority, and most of the vegetables we used came from the garden. Early and main crop peas, beans and cabbages were planted, as were runner beans. In the spring the root crops like carrots, swedes and beetroot were grown along with onions from sets, spring onions and other salad type items. Along with all of the digging and ground prepara-tion, the chemical Elsan toilets had to be emptied, but it is not wise to dwell too long on this subject, though needless to say we always had a good crop of sprouts. We had good neighbours who I could ask about gardening queries etc. I seemed to get good results for all of the effort and became a dab hand with a hack and a dutch hoe.

At this time we decided to keep chickens, so a portion of our shed was partitioned off to form a nesting and roosting area; this was shut off each night to keep the foxes out. Outside the nesting area a portion of the garden was fenced off with chicken wire (mesh) to allow the poten-tial egg producers to wander around and scratch for worms. After all of this preparation work we got the chickens. 'One day old chicks'. It seemed an eternity before they resembled what we wanted, but with patience and some fall out, we got the pullets' eggs and then on to the real full size eggs. This allowed us to have eggs for most of the year round. We also got some male chicks for food purposes, but when the due time came, I couldn't face the dispatch part and 'chickened out' so

Bob in National Service   Bob and Gordon

outside help had to be obtained.

In the early part of the war we were all given Anderson shelters for protection. These were sunk four feet into the ground, and then concreted in and covered with earth. If the siren went off we would all get out of bed and troop down to the shelter, and stay there until the 'all clear' went or even stay there all night. This was so disruptive, smelly and damp that most people decided against going to the shelter at all. They seemed to favour going into the cupboard under the stairs until it was all over.

Church attendance was also important at this time, and most young boys at that time became choir members. There was choir practice on Thursday evenings and the real thing for Matins on Sunday morning, plus the evening service. Some boys dropped out along the way, but some kept going. It certainly helped at Christmas, because we knew and had rehearsed all of the carols, so we made a very good show and sound as carol singers.

Schooling during this time was also rather disjointed, because if the sirens went during school hours we all went to a large shelter in the school grounds until the end of the raid. Most of the teachers also did Air Raid Warden duties, so some of them may have been up all night doing this and then have to teach a class the next day. (Sometimes a little fraught!) I still have the scars to prove it.

To help at certain times of the year (especially harvest time), we would go to local farms to help with the potato crop. A coach would be at the school at 9 am, and we would be taken to a farm in the area to pick and sack the potatoes. We would have a break for lunch and be back at school for 4.30 pm. This would be typical for a period lasting several weeks. We also used to help the farmers do their hay making, but this was in our own time as at that time of year the days were long, and we also had double summer time. We all felt that we were helping the war effort, and it didn't seem to matter that we were losing our childhood and education. At other times of the year we used to gather rose hips and take them to school where they were collected, and made into rose hip syrup; this was then supplied to infants etc. We also used to collect conkers, and take them to school where they were sent away to be made into cattle feed. This was harder to get to grips with, because it is very hard for a boy to give up his conkers.

During the war, it did not occur to me that I was unlucky or missing anything. However, later in life I did wonder why all of my contemporaries had their fathers at home for this period of time (I can only think of one other head of household who was called up for service in HM forces). It turned an 8-year boy into a 12-year old man.

With the storage tanks completed, and the terminal now working at the bottom of the hill, the road traffic built up tremendously. 'Pool Petrol' tanker lorries were arriving, filling and delivering petrol to all parts of the South West non-stop. This seemed to generate more of everything. The milkman started to deliver milk in bottles, the baker came round to your door with a large basket of various sized loaves (a cottage loaf was very popular). The ironmonger also came round once a week to your door with supplies of paraffin, matches, cleaning items and all manner of hardware goods.

The nearest shopping area was Westbury, which is where all of the trams stopped at the terminus. They would go into town, but unfortunately would not come any closer to Henbury so all provisions had to be carried the old fashioned way. A grocer on Westbury Hill, J. H. Mills would however deliver to your home, so you went to the shop to select and pay for your goods and it would be delivered to your home on a certain day. Supplies from the butcher and greengrocer had to be carried in the usual way.

Conker collecting at Henbury School

Towards the end of the war, there were more mechanical contraptions about. The day of the bus had arrived, which did not need rails to run on. I can still remember that the seats were very hard and they had very poor suspensions. If the bus went too fast over the hump back bridge near the Salutation Hotel it became 'air borne'. Anyway the driver seemed to enjoy it even if the passengers didn't.

Early after the war, developments started to happen at a very rapid rate such as house building. Arnall Drive was the first area to be started in this vast building programme. I can remember standing on the top of the church tower to look across at the first swathe of land being removed, to start the Arnall Drive road. We remarked that this was a landmark in our own history, but little did I know in the late 1940s how significant that statement would be. I later met my lovely wife Lyn (formerly Evelyn Taylor) here at Arnall Drive and we have now been married for 50 years.

From 1951 to 52 I was in the army doing National Service as did most

Bob and Lyn with mum and dad Steer

young men of that age.

At this time everything was moving at a fast rate. Houses both private and council were going ahead, cars and other transport were increasing rapidly, as was the aircraft business at nearby Filton where they were building the Britannia aeroplane. Many of the people living at Henbury worked at either the BAC aircraft engine dept. (now Rolls Royce) or BAC aircraft (now BAe Systems).

1954 saw me marry my lovely Lyn at Henbury church, where we had both been church bell ringers.

1964 saw us emigrate to Ontario Canada.

1977 saw us return to Henbury, where we have lived on the old Convent site for 28 years.

I state 'the old Convent site' to identify it for most people, but I remember it as pasture fields, long before the Convent was built.

Reflections

On reflection the years between the 1930s and the 1950s were the start of all the major changes that we have seen in village life. Until then Henbury was a 'village community', with its own church and infrastructure, and a mother church for the larger Parish of surrounding villages: Hallen, Compton Greenfield (now Easter Compton) and Charlton (now vanished under the Brabazon runway). Beyond the Parish, Almonsbury, Olveston, Pilning, Elberton and Littleton-on-Severn were self-contained, but also part of the bigger, rural community.

In researching my family tree I found that from around 1800, my earliest research to date, to the 1930s, four generations of my mother's family were born, lived and died in the Parish. (The only exception was my great grandmother who was born in Thornbury in 1844 and, at 21, married and settled in Almondsbury. She had five children and was widowed at 36. She married again, had a second family, and died in Hallen in 1928). It struck me that this type of close community prevailed right up until the 30s. After that, from the 30s to the 50s, changes happened quickly but the community spirit still strongly prevailed; in the 60s and beyond occured most of the changes we see today.

Another Community?

Not strictly in Henbury village, but in some respects forming its own small community is the 'King William' Inn, affectionately known as the 'King Billy'. Here you could find, over many years, Henbury villagers collecting together after an arduous day in the fields, at craft work, at business or trade. It is appropriate I believe to remember the proprietor of the 'King Billy' then (and now) Ken Lane, a friendly and popular man. He was not a Henbury boy but in his growing up years he was closely associated with the village.

Kenneth Lane was born in March 1925 at Lane's Dairy, Filton Hill. After the death of his mother when he was three years old (his father died when he was six) a Mrs Benson took him to live at The Fox in Easter Compton where he attended the nearby Infants school. In 1932 when Ken was seven years old, the Bensons became landlords of the 'King Billy' in Hallen.

Ken's schooling then continued at Henbury Boys School in Church Close. At that time, the Headmaster was Mr Denis Smart, his deputy was Mr Dai Davies, and among the other teachers were Miss Park and Miss Brown. Ken took his midday meal with four or five other boys in the conservatory behind Mrs Tinknell's shop in the village street – opposite the Post Office. Before he left school at the age of fourteen, he was Captain of School, and had studied general subjects but no languages. Ken says he thoroughly enjoyed his schooldays.

On leaving school, he went to work for Mr Collard. Opposite the 'King Billy' was a village shop and Post Office. Behind the shop was Collard's farm. Ken took on the job of helping in the cow sheds, getting the cows in and out for milking. Milk was delivered to doorsteps, the householder providing a jug for the milk that was then ladled from the farmer's churn.

As Ken was starting his life of work, war broke out in 1939 when he was fourteen years old. He soon joined the Home Guard. Tom Hignell of Norton Farm, a few years his senior was paired with Ken to patrol various areas including the entrance to the Severn tunnel. To begin with, they were armed with pitchfork and rifle, but no bullets!

Mr Benson died in 1941 leaving his wife to look after the 'King Billy'. When Ken was seventeen and a half years old, he joined the Royal Navy. In 1947 after war service with the Navy, Ken became landlord of the 'King Billy'. In his spare time, he played for the Hallen and Henbury Football Association, and won a cup, in a tournament at the Rovers Ground. He also played cricket and golf, rode his bike and walked miles to Henbury, Westbury etc. He remembers attending local events especially the Hallen and Henbury Flower Show.

In the early nineteen seventies, Ken married Jacky Mackay whose grandparents lived at Wyck House in Henbury. Ken and Jacky have one son named Martin.

At the 'King Billy', they served beer and stout (porter). There is an ancient brewhouse attached to the pub where beer was brewed on the premises. Opposite was St John's Church and Church Infants School. There was also

Ken and Jacky Lane

a Baptist Chapel built about 1832. Coal was an important commodity and was purchased from Brown (Arthur) and Goodfield (George), operating at Henbury Station Yard.

In 2003, Ken received an award of a silver tankard and a portrait of himself to hang in the 'King Billy' from the brewery company 'Inspired'. His 56 years as Landlord made him the longest serving licensee of the Company.

6

Families who came to Henbury during the late nineteenth and early twentieth centuries

Gunn, Adridge, Budgett, James, Langfield

The families in this chapter came to the village about the end of the nineteenth or beginning of the twentieth century. They were comfortably off and were able to provide employment to a number of villagers. According to many contributors to this study there was a good relationship between employers and employed with much kindness and friendship on both sides.

The Gunn Family of Henbury House: a personal memoir

The Gunns believe that Henbury House dates from about 1760. However the family traces its ancestry to the Norse Vikings. The Henbury family descended from Rev. John Gun who left Caithness c.1800 and became a Congregational Minister in Chard. (The second 'n' was added to the name 'Gun' around 1800 when the hand gun superseded the blunderbuss.) Rev John married the daughter of a West India merchant who died at sea. Her inheritance of £10,000 was lost in a failed investment shortly after her husband's death in 1836. She was left with a large family to educate.

The eldest son, another Minister, struggled to pay off the family debts, and then sadly his wife died. He married again to the eldest daughter of H.0. Wills II, the tobacco entrepreneur. Their son Henry (Harry) Wills Gunn, a qualified accountant, traded successfully in the East until he was invalided home in 1883.

Harry was unemployed up until 1897 when Wills became mechanized and expanded – and offered employment to their cousins. He soon settled in, becoming first Secretary of Wills, and in 1901 of the Imperial Tobacco Company. After that things improved for him, but he never forgot the problems of being unemployed and hard up.

Harry Gunn and his wife Lilias Sommerville set up house at Elmfield in Westbury on Trym. Their son Henry Sommerville Gunn (known as Sommer-

The Gunn Family tree

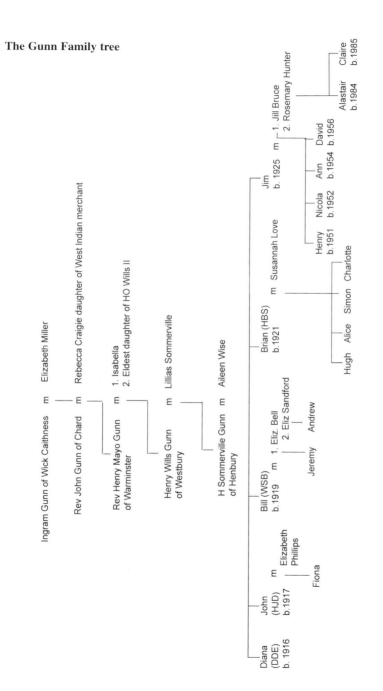

Ingram Gunn of Wick Caithness m Elizabeth Miller

Rev John Gunn of Chard m Rebecca Craigie daughter of West Indian merchant

Rev Henry Mayo Gunn of Warminster m 1. Isabella
2. Eldest daughter of HO Wills II

Henry Wills Gunn of Westbury m Lillias Sommerville

H Sommerville Gunn of Henbury m Aileen Wise

Diana (DDE) b. 1916

John (HJD) b.1917 m Elizabeth Phillips

Fiona

Bill (WSB) b.1919 m 1. Eliz. Bell
2. Eliz Sandford

Jeremy   Andrew

Brian (HBS) b.1921 m Susannah Love

Hugh Alice Simon Charlotte

Jim b. 1925 m 1. Jill Bruce
2. Rosemary Hunter

Henry b.1951   Nicola b.1952   Ann b.1954   David b.1956

Alastair b.1984   Claire b.1985

ville) in 1914 married Aileen Wise of Lustleigh, South Devon whose Wise ancestors came from Waterford, and whose paternal grandmother Maria Dymock was a god daughter of Hannah More.

Francis Wise, a cousin of Aileen's, had a whiskey distillery in Cork and gave a donation for the Finbars Cathedral to be built by William Burges.

In 1921 after living in Stoke Bishop, Sommerville and Aileen Gunn moved to Henbury House the year their fourth child Brian was born. Here the children grew up and enjoyed a happy country childhood.

James, the fifth and youngest child, describes the house as interesting. He thinks that Edmund Burke of parliamentary fame (and friend of Harford) scratched his name on the upstairs sitting room window. He remembers a smoking room, its heyday probably about 1890 when Turkish cigarettes were smoked. His mother 'heated' it with a peat fire which gave out a lot of dust and not much heat! But it smelled nice.

When the Gunns moved into Henbury House, there was only gas lighting, but when electricity was later installed, H.S. Gunn had one gas light retained over his armchair – he thought it gave a better light. In those days between-the-wars, coal was still the main fuel for heating water and warming the house. For this purpose they had a boiler in the cellar which had to be filled with coal. Arthur Williams did this, and it provided hot water, and heated one radiator occasionally – no other central heating! Fires, if any, in the rooms were coal and wood. Rainwater was collected from the roof into a tank beneath the house. A water softener filled with salt kept the pies in good condition.

In time drains were replaced by modern pipes, probably in preparation for the proposed housing estates, the previous brick conduits along Henbury Road had probably drained into the brook (I imagine this was 'clean' drainage). There was a reed bed or lake which may have been where the sewage drain ended.

There was a small building adjoining Henbury House, complete with kitchen, servants' hall and two maids' rooms in the upper storey. It was joined to the house by a wooden corridor. Brian writes, 'I well remember

Henbury House

our cook Mrs Nelmes who lived in one of these rooms while two maids occupied another.'

For many years now, this building has been known as 'Canteen Cottage', a name derived from the time of the second world war when Mrs Gunn set it up as a canteen for the armed forces, and other war workers stationed in Henbury. Joan Wellington, who with her mother lived at The Hollies, managed the canteen.

A large house and garden, and a family of five children entails a good deal of work, and the Gunns were sufficiently well-off to employ staff to do this. Diana writes,

> There is a memorial stone on the wall in the churchyard to Sarah Ross, 'NANA'. She was our nanny for many years, presiding over the nursery at the top of the house. She came from Glasgow, Scottish and very strict when we wore 'the kilt' to parties. One of her previous 'babies' Humphrey Kemp, by then a clergyman, came to see her before she died. She was part of the family.

Brian comments,

Beyond the green baize door, the house was 'home' to the staff. Mrs

Sommerville and Aileen Gunn and family

Nelmes vetted very carefully any young girls wanting a 'position'. The good name of the house was vital. Mrs Nelmes was just like Mrs Bridges in 'Upstairs Downstairs'.

James says that looking back he remembers the staff as highly trained able people at a time when being 'in service' was a well regarded profession.

As well as Nana and Bass (Edith Bassett) in the nursery, Woodsford the chauffeur was a first rate engineer who could not only keep the cars running but was good company to every member of the family. He had the knack of saying whatever was needed, and I think coined the phrase 'positional' to describe an easy relationship. Then there was Williams, under gardener to Brice. Upstanding and strong and a good footballer, one always felt safe with him around.

There were the grooms too… Poundsbury, and his twins… and Mrs Culley, who had been in the nursery before Bass… all these are among my warmest memories of childhood, and I enjoyed seeing them again later.

Diana adds,

Mr Scutt, seeing Brian being dragged through a thick hedge or Kitty on a leading rein, shouted 'you'll kill that child Mrs Gunn', and her answer 'that's all right Mr Scutt, I have plenty more at home'. The stables and garage, and gardener's cottage were at the far end of the garden where 'Henbury Gardens' is now. The Poundsbury Family lived in the bungalow behind The Elms Farmhouse. He had been groom in the Berkeley Kennels and recommended by Will Morris the Huntsman – who also recommended Bill Adlam on Mendip to sell us a horse for Pah – the horse got the name 'gatecrasher'.

The Gunn family loved dogs and horses. Diana also remembers,

> …Bill bursting into tears when the sheep dog puppy that was to be his, arrived at Henbury Station, having travelled by train from Bovey Tracey. It was in a basket with a lid, and he said, "they have bent his tail.' This dog Bill named 'Help', saying if he was in trouble, he would just call 'Help'!

They spent a number of summer holidays in Devon to be near their Wise grandparents and great grandmother Maria Wise (Dymock) at Lustleigh. John got on well with Gaffer who had been in the Indian Forestry service. They were keen naturalists with butterfly collections. They stayed on Dartmoor, taking ponies, dogs and musical instruments with them, and rode on the Moor or sailed and swam at Shaldon. On those occasions, they sent their ponies by train from Henbury Station, journeying themselves by car in the bull-nosed Morris. They met the ponies at Bovey Station, and rode them up to Haytor.

Father Sommerville, when 'Imperial' made Saturday a regular day off, hunted with the Berkeley Hounds, as indeed did the whole family. His other interests were golf, being an active member at Failand and he served as Master of the Society of Merchant Venturers. Diana accompanied him to some of the social events because, sadly, their mother fell victim to Meniers disease that severely affected her hearing. This was particularly tragic as she was a gifted musician. Gaffer had sent her to the Royal College of Music to study violin, and said 'it was the happiest two years of my life, then I got married!' Poor Pah – she teased him. She was a member of the Bristol Music Club. Their friends, the Napier Miles lived in Kings Weston House. Mr Miles was musical too, and they played quartets together. Diana remembers a meeting of the Berkeley Hounds at Kings Weston House.

Brian used to walk the dogs in Blaise Woods. He remembers Mrs Pearce in her romantic thatched cottage with walls covered in cork bark, warm and cosy always welcoming and the time the cow fell through the roof – 'she stayed with us during repairs.'

Older residents of Henbury remember Aileen Gunn as a woman of considerable character and determination. She made herself aware of needs not only in the village but in the wider community, then set about the task of rectifying them.

Diana remembers,

> She was on committees of Bristol Children's Orthopaedic Hospital, which was then in Grove Road Redland. She ran a sewing group at Henbury House to make red bed jackets and other clothing for the children who were often in 'traction'. Then she had a bed rigged up on our pony trap with my pony, Wendy. One of my dolls was put into 'traction' on the bed, and driven around Bristol to collect money for what eventually became Winford Hospital. The children mostly suffered from ricketts, due it is believed to a shortage of milk during the war. She also started an egg run, because the hospital could not afford to give children fresh eggs. In this scheme people gave as many eggs as they could afford, some giving up to a dozen a week. Aileen would drive round in the pony trap to collect them, and afterwards deliver them to the children.

One of her notable Henbury interests was the Henbury Robins Football Team recalled with much affection by the 'boys' themselves in their elderly years. Arthur Williams was a great goalie.

The Gunn children had friends of their own locally: for instance, the Sampson Ways, the Ways, Budgetts, the Aldridges. They had friends among the farmers, Mr Grigg the blacksmith and many others. James had as companions, when he was quite young, two cousins whose parents were serving abroad, and who were left for a time with their relatives. He also liked to range around the woods and the village where he made friends with the Schoolmaster, unkindly and unjustly nicknamed, 'Bloody Old Smarty'. James remembers that he gave him a wedding present, so they must have kept in touch. James pictures him 'outside the School near the grave of Scipio Africanus, with the peacocks crying in the background.'

James also vividly remembers the air raid on Bristol when the night sky over Blaise woods was brilliantly lit up and bright red,

> With Bristol being bombed the guns were serviced by ATS girls on range finders. They lived in tents and got cold so the Billeting officer came round looking for rooms. Ma said she would take 30 or 40 if the all highest agreed. He did and they moved in quite quickly. A few weeks later a girl got scarlet fever, a notifiable disease. Ma had to report it to the medical officer of health who said 'please keep her, all Bristol hospitals are full'. That is how Henbury House Hospital began.

Brian says,

> Christmas that year was fun and very exciting. She became a St Johns Ambulance nurse and was helped by volunteers, had a flair for diagnosis and an ongoing game with the MO…What have you got for me today Mrs Gunn?

During her three and a half years in this role, Princess Mary, the Princess Royal as chief commandant paid an official visit. James and Brian both remember another visit from Royalty. This was when Winford Hospital was opened about 1929. James aged about 4 and Brian 8 presented purses to the Queen Mother, when she was Duchess of York. Brian says he remembers the white daisies in the field known as the Royals, when Billy Budget was making hay. Also walks down the vicarage steps, up through the tunnel, past Canon Way's grave to the Post Office. Visits to the Soap Bowl, Gorams Chair and Lovers Leap were also exciting. The water mill had been rescued from Chew Valley in Somerset when the lake was built. He still has the cufflinks that Larley Sampson Way gave him as page at her wedding. 'We knew Abigail Way', says Brian, 'she called her children Diana and Brian.'

Brian adds,

> My bedroom window faced the church and the chimes of its eight bells

rang across on a Friday evening. I always knew when a new comer was learning change ringing.

Aileen and her children worshipped at All Saints Church in Clifton. It was high church and rudely referred to as 'all smells and bells'. I was made to admit that I erred and strayed like a lost sheep which was not a bit popular, but the music, vestments and ceremony were wonderful. However, they all attended the Christmas day service at St Mary's Church, Henbury because their father preferred it. Jim, aged 5, during the Sermon was heard to say in a loud whisper, 'Mummy, I have heard all this before'.

After the war the family moved, the parents went to Box Cottage at Tormarton. Henbury House was divided into flats and sold after Sommerville died in 1966. John returned to England from Nigeria and his wife Elizabeth became ill. Retiring from the army, he lived in part of the house and grew strawberries. He used cloches and sold his fruit several weeks before others. He then moved to Didmarton.

When building was begun on the Henbury gardens site, a tunnel was found roofed in lead. Originally the tunnel was used by the gardener to wheel rubbish into the kitchen garden without being seen. Jim remarked 'good place for children to hide'.

The five children of Sommerville and Aileen considered themselves fortunate in their parents who were temperamentally very different. Characteristics which passed on to later generations. They were gifted in various ways, Diana studied at the Royal College of Music and Jim was musical too. Though they were not brilliant in school, they passed their exams and enjoyed games.

John had an Exmoor pony, Puffin, which he rode bareback and schooled to a high standard, now called dressage. After Sandhurst he joined the Royal Scots Greys, played polo and went with the grey horses to Palestine. Later they had tanks, fought at Alamein and at Solerno in Italy, and from Normandy John led his Squadron to Wizmar on the Baltic Sea. He gained an MC.

Bill trained at Woolwich, joined the Royal Artillery and went to Algiers where he received its surrender. He gained an MC in Italy, served with the King's Troop, commanded a regiment in Germany and settled at Ilmington.

Brian served with KRRC in North Africa, Italy and Europe, then he went to Cambridge, became a Civil Engineer, but being a bit deaf retired to Winscombe to farm.

Jim served in the RA in India, went to Oxford, and then worked for Players. He became High Sheriff of Nottingham. 'Clan Gunn' was his hobby.

Diana served with the Wrens, and then attended Barnett House to train for Social Work, mostly with university chaplaincies. She taught the violin to children. She now lives at St Monica's home where she does the flowers in the chapel which she watched being built when she was at Badminton in 1922. They had all been to Badminton, then the boys to Avondale near Clifton College and to boarding school at Durnford near Swanage. There they played games and swam at 'dancing ledge', a smugglers' cove.

> Pa sent us to Durnford because the Deputy Head Arthur Worsely had been his cricket captain at Malvern. At fathers' match it was 'ah Gunn, second slip as usual please'. His ancient 'whites' were held up by his Gloucestershire Gypsy tie. We were teased.

Jim was always known as Jim at home but his wife thinks 'James' sounds more positional. This short account of a Henbury family offers yet another insight into country life and relationships between families, their neighbours and employees within the village. Such relationships seem to give pleasure to all concerned.

A Mr Jack Burrell writes that he is a member of the Clifton Cricket Club, except the club plays on a field on Henbury Hill which he believes belongs to Mr Gunn of Henbury House. Jim confirms this and says that it was compulsorily purchased when the housing estate was built. Compensation was paid for loss of value to Henbury House because its view was spoiled and a strip of field was left undeveloped.

The Aldridges of Chesterfield House
In the Census of 1891, Charles and Lucy Aldridge are listed as living with their children and two servants at Chesterfield House. In *Kelly's Trade*

Directory of 1931, Miss Aldridge (Mabel) is listed as Honorary Secretary to the Henbury Nursing Association. Her mother at that time was Head of Household.

From a short correspondence with Miss Elizabeth Osborn, and later with her nephew Mark Osborn, it was possible to write a paragraph and draw a limited family-tree. The house, so beautiful in its commanding position at the top of Henbury Hill, was known to locals as 'the chest of drawers house' because of its shape. It is still a landmark, and nowadays is a house with surrounding flats. But in the intervening years since the Aldridges left, and before its present renaissance it had a varied use. During the war it suffered fire damage, and later was used as a night club. It is therefore interesting to catch at least a small glimpse of the house as a family home.

Charles and Lucy Aldridge

Elizabeth Osborn sadly died before our correspondence was completed, something that she herself would have regretted because she loved the house, and wanted other people to know what it was like. Elizabeth wrote from her home near Newton Abbot,

I was delighted to receive your letter, and to learn of your project connected with Henbury. I shall be very glad to help you in any way that I can about Chesterfield House and the surrounding area, in my childhood before 1939. My grandparents, Charles and Lucy Aldridge, lived at Chesterfield House, and I have very happy memories of it all. I loved every corner, and still do! We three children of Dora, the youngest daughter of Charles and Lucy were frequent visitors, gamely trudging from Downleaze, with my mother

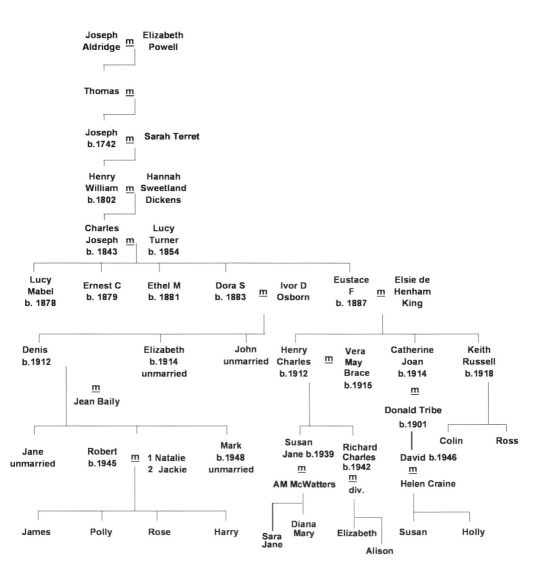

Joseph Aldridge **m** Elizabeth Powell

Thomas **m**

Joseph b.1742 **m** Sarah Terret

Henry William b.1802 **m** Hannah Sweetland Dickens

Charles Joseph b. 1843 **m** Lucy Turner b. 1854

Lucy Mabel b. 1878 — Ernest C b. 1879 — Ethel M b. 1881 — Dora S b. 1883 **m** Ivor D Osborn — Eustace F b. 1887 **m** Elsie de Henham King

Denis b.1912 — Elizabeth b.1914 unmarried — John unmarried — Henry Charles b.1912 **m** Vera May Brace b.1915 — Catherine Joan b.1914 **m** — Keith Russell b.1918

m Jean Baily

Donald Tribe b.1901

Jane unmarried — Robert b.1945 **m** 1 Natalie 2 Jackie — Mark b.1948 unmarried

Susan Jane b.1939 **m** AM McWatters — Richard Charles b.1942 **m** div.

David b.1946 **m** Helen Craine

Colin — Ross

James — Polly — Rose — Harry

Sara Jane — Diana Mary

Elizabeth

Alison

Susan — Holly

115

Chesterfield House

pushing a pram with small son, the other boy on a bicycle, and myself hauling along the dog, a rather portly Sealyham. In those days, we could cut through by Westbury on Trym by lanes and fields for the most part.

Since the previous paragraphs were written, Mark Osborn suggested speaking to Mrs Joan Tribe, daughter of Eustace Aldridge, and granddaughter of Charles and Lucy. Joan Tribe remembers with pleasure her visits to Chesterfield House when she and her parents and brothers would walk from their house in Southfield Road, Westbury on Trym up to the top of Henbury hill.

There were occasions when my grandparents Charles and Lucy gathered together their large family, and we enjoyed meeting our cousins. In my memory, the house was lit with gas mantles. In winter it was very cold, especially on the top floor. Of course there were coal fires but the heat did not penetrate into the corners of the rooms. I remember little about the servants, except that every morning they assembled with the family in the breakfast room for prayers. This room was to the left of the front door as you entered the house. To the right was a very large and long dining room with a dais at the far end. The large drawing room that overlooked the garden and fields had a 'D' shaped (Nash) window, and to the left, a large conservatory filled with exotic ferns that grandpa was very proud of, and out of bounds to children! The kitchen and 'boot room' were along a corridor behind the breakfast room. The kitchen was a large room, and when I was a child visiting the house, the aunts seemed to be doing the cooking. They were very good but the maids were probably helping.

Joan Tribe went on to describe how important the surroundings of the house were to her:

There was a very long stretch of garden inside the stone wall that ran along Henbury hill to Tramore, and at the end of this was a large greenhouse that was filled with grapevines. Then there was the fruit garden next to it with raspberries, gooseberries and other fruit. Peaches grew on the red brick wall; the fruit was so warm and soft when plucked by eager young hands. But the gardener Mr Horseman whose cottage was across the road below Henbury Hill House, reigned supreme in his garden, and woe betide any family members who did not seek his permission. In this part of the gardens, there was also a large lily pond.

There was a ha ha to keep animals out because the Budgett family kept cows on the adjacent fields. We had fun in these fields picking enormous bunches of cowslips and making them into balls and throwing them at each other.

To the north of the house was a tennis court and a large lawn that reached round the back. To the south there were fields that Charles and Lucy had sold in 1895 to the Henbury golf club.

Grandfather Charles had a business importing steel and iron. The premises were in Marsh Street in Bristol City. He used to travel to his business by pony and trap and his daughters also travelled to be educated at Badminton School in this way.

Joan Tribe relates how Charles and Lucy had a stern attitude to behaviour on Sundays and they were not allowed to read anything except the Bible.

In the evening they would gather around the piano and sing hymns. Within this beautiful house and gardens there was plenty of space for children and grandchildren to play; and a grand sense of 'family' was created by Charles and Lucy.

The Budgett Family of Tramore

The Budgett family has been associated with Tramore House (the name quoted in documents at that time) since 1885 when Mrs Georgiana Elsie Budgett agreed to rent the house. The agreement was for seven years at a rent of £70 per annum with option to renew for a further seven years. But it seems that some time a little later, the house was purchased by the Budgett Family.

It seems that H.H. Budgett and his family took up residence there in about 1948. Their daughter Mrs Julie Bate writes that they lived there until 1969 after which they moved to the New Forest. Henbury villagers remember this family well not least because their Jersey herd was a great feature of village life. The herd browsed on fields known as 'The Royals', behind the house. There is a mention of 'Royall Way' in the deeds of the house though it is not clear if this refers to Henbury Road.

Julie Bate writes about her house and family,

> I believe that the original cottage was a hunting lodge (the deeds go back to 1680). When we were first there, the old kitchen and all of the original 'cottage' area had flag stone floors. The cellar was constantly flooding, and under the new kitchen was a natural well from which we used to pump cold water into the stone sink in the scullery to clean the vegetables.

> I well remember Mr Bray who was incidentally our gardener, not the hen keeper. [In a previous Henbury book, a villager remembered him as such.] My parents had the Jersey cow herd until the early 1950s when they were sold. The milk was cooled in the dairy in our back garden and then went to Biggs for pasteurization. We owned The Royalls to the boundary of the Blaise woods, and also all the adjoining fields to the boundary of Chesterfield House.

There were cow sheds next to what we called the 'Top Garden' which had a boundary from the lane cut through outside our garden wall along the main road (Henbury Road). We grew peaches and plums along the inside wall. It was always very hot. There was also a greenhouse in which we grew grapes. The 'bottom garden' was indeed inside a boundary wall by the Salutation pub; and all the way up the walk from the ford to the boundary of the Wills' house (The Old Vicarage).

We did at one time have geese, pigs and hens in this area. I remember the potato peelings etc being boiled up in a special boiler in the coach house giving off a distinctively revolting aroma! We also had an enormous green house with roses, vines and other plants – this had a huge water well in the middle which I suppose was fed by the Hen. We grew red, white and black currants in what seemed an enormous area to me. This land was eventually sold to build the present houses.

Like many other residents of rural and semi-rural Henbury, H.H. Budgett recently died, but thanks to his daughter there is this record of their time here.

The James Family of Hill End

Hill End was the home of the James family from 1928/9 until the early years of the war. To many people nowadays, Hill End is merely a road name. That it had been a flourishing small country estate is vividly explained by Major John James, who also provides a paragraph about the Strattons of Severn House.

Mr James writes,

My father Gilbert Sidney James, who had worked for Imperial Tobacco before World War I, went off to the war in the Royal Artillery in 1914, and when the war was over, returned to work in the tobacco industry in Bristol where his father had worked before him.

The earliest childhood home I can remember was in Weston-super-Mare. We moved to Hill End when I was rising six. When we first moved in, mains electricity had yet to reach Henbury. In a large row of sheds behind the house, was a generator which charged up a big bank of accumulators to provide light for the house. The system occasionally

Hill End

failed and it was back to candles and lamps again until it could be fixed. In the main, the house was kept warm(ish) by open fires or oil heaters as far as I can remember. A couple of years later mains electricity arrived, and soon after that electric fires and oil-fired central heating.

Henbury in those days was pretty well entirely rural. Quite a lot of land went with Hill End, and in the early 1930s, additional grazing ground was rented so as to accommodate both some horses and a small number of Guernsey cattle to provide milk and butter for the house.

Except for a walled vegetable garden at the highest point of the grounds, when we first got to Hill End, the garden was pretty rough – or so it seems in my memory now. In the early thirties quite a lot of landscaping was done; I have since understood that my father had this

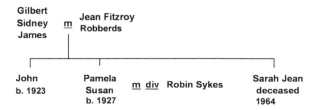

Pamela and Sarah James

done in part to make work during the high unemployment of the Depression. It of course also enhanced the property. My father also had two or possibly three small houses built nearby for people working at Hill End. I think a local builder called Mr Harvey did the house building – but my memory may be faulty on this.

I think the cattle were the first livestock to be brought in. They were looked after by Mr Elton, and were housed, and milked, by hand, in shedding at the back of the vegetable garden. Mrs Elton did the dairying in a building near the stable block which, years later together with the stables, was demolished to clear the ground for the laundry to be built by the Nuns. Mr and Mrs Elton lived in the lodge at the entrance to the Hill End drive.

Fairly soon after the cattle came, a pony was bought for me apparently because some doctor had said riding would help to correct incipient knock-knees! At first Elton looked after the pony as well as the cows. Soon, a not very good looking heavy old hunter was got in so that Elton could keep up with me as I got more confident. Then my mother took to riding and became a fine and brave horsewoman.

Mrs James, a fine horsewoman

During the first war, my father as a Battery Commander in the Artillery, had had much to do with horses, and not to be outdone, took up riding again, and ultimately played Polo on a ground at Filton. (With the Second World War, the Polo ground disappeared under the Bristol Aircraft Company factory.) In the end a bit of horse-breeding went on at Hill End as well. By 1938, we must have had a dozen assorted ponies, horses, brood mares on the property, and these were looked after by Andrew Painter, whose wife Minnie had been my sisters' nurse maid, and later was Mrs Sims' mother.

In the school holidays, riding every day, more or less regardless of the weather was the standard routine, and a main activity of our lives. I certainly accepted it as a matter of course, rather like bread and butter at tea! Looking back on it now, it was a happy and healthy time, and I got to know the surrounding countryside as far away as Tockington quite well as a result of exercising horses, going to gymkhanas and so on. In those days, I rode for miles around Henbury, all then open country, usually with Andrew Painter, sometimes with my mother and occasionally with my father. As they got older, my sisters joined in these expeditions, too. I remember Hounds meeting on the edge of Moorgrove, a stone's throw from Hill End, in about 1932, and riding in the children's class more than once at Henbury Show.

Another riding memory is going with Andrew Painter to the Blacksmith in Easter Compton to have the horses re-shod, both of us riding one horse and leading another. The blacksmith was called Mr Purnell and I remember pumping the forge bellows, and the smell of singeing when very hot shoes were settled on to freshly trimmed hooves. As well as being the blacksmith, Mr Purnell ran the Easter Compton Brass Band. At Christmas time, they used to come over to Henbury, and play carols, collecting funds, I imagine for the Band Fund. At Hill End, they came into the hall after playing and were given alcoholic drinks, coffee and buns before going on to their next port of call.

For my first year at Henbury, I went to school at Badminton Kinder-garten, and after that to a little day school in Henleaze for a couple of years. I was dropped off at school sometimes by my father on his way to work, and sometimes by my mother or a chauffeur. I was dropped on the edge of Henleaze to walk the last bit to school so that I was properly awake at the start of lessons! In consequence, most of the friends of my own age were Henleaze boys, and a couple of boys called Bethel from a farm between Hallen and Easter Compton with whom I used to ride.

Early memories of going to school in Henleaze remind me that Falcondale Road was as yet unbuilt, and that on the way to school we went through Westbury on Trym, past the War Memorial and tram ter-minus, and that my mother's Austin Seven tended to get its wheels caught in the tram lines if she wasn't careful. I think that in 1930 I used to get 6d. per week pocket money, and used to buy sweeties at the store opposite the entrance to Blaise Castle.

I went off to boarding school in Cirencester in the autumn of 1933, so Henbury childhood contacts became fewer. I did get to know the Gunn family through riding, though mostly they were older than me. Jim Gunn is the one I remember best as he was a great competitor at Pony Club events. The other Gunn children were several years older than I so I never got to know them very well.

The Stratton family lived in Severn House a few hundred yards across a little valley from us. There were three children in that family,

Prudence who was much the same age as me, Rosemary, a little younger than me, and a younger brother David who was quite a lot younger than the rest of us. Until about 1935 we hardly ever met, but around then, Prudence and Rosemary became interested in riding, and for the next two or three years we became good friends, as I used to go over and help them with their ponies fairly frequently in the school holidays. There was a large pond in their field alongside the Hallen road which was good for skating on in the winter. We seemed to have a lot of hard winters in those days. One summer shortly before the war, Rosemary was tragically drowned in a swimming accident somewhere when the Stratton family were away on summer holiday.

Somewhere around 1935/6 my father started taking me out rough shooting with him, and I was put under the charge of a Mr Davis, who I believe was a local poacher in his spare time, to learn how to be safe with a gun. It was quite a long time before I was allowed to carry any ammunition – for a start, only an empty gun was allowed. We knew a tenant farmer called Mr Shepherd and his wife who farmed on the south west side of Hallen, and on whose land there was an extensive rabbit warren where we sometimes went ferreting.

You will gather from all this 'rambling on' that we lived a very open air and active sort of life which must have been very healthy and good for us. I never had a great liking for school, and sometimes struggled with exams. This reminds me of the Vicar Mr Lloyd who was a good friend of my parents and whose church we regularly attended. In spring 1937 I was expected to fail the entrance exam for Marlborough College – Latin was one of my worst subjects – and the Vicar's son Raymond was an expert in languages. I was sent by my anxious parents to the Vicarage two or three mornings a week to be crammed in Latin by Raymond during the Easter holidays that year! I passed the exams.

In 1938 huge underground fuel tanks and petrol pipelines along with a railway spur were put in just below the house on the Avonmouth side which worried my parents. The war was looming, and these seemed to present an obvious target and we were right on the edge of it. There was talk of moving house but nothing was done. At that time, my father was a Squadron Leader in the Royal Auxiliary Air Force, commanding one of the three Aux. A F Balloon Barrage Squadrons intended for the defence of Bristol. In summer 1939 we were on holiday in Devon when the Reserves were mobilised, and we all came home. My father's Squadron was deployed around Avonmouth, and for a short time, he used Hill End as his Squadron H.Q.

Around Christmas 1939 a party of Government Surveyors arrived on our doorstep, and announced that they would be taking over the property for some RAF purpose in the late spring. We had to pack up and move out quite quickly. We moved to a large bungalow in Stoke Bishop, and later to a rented house near Bridgwater. So you will see that I lived at Hill End between the ages of six and sixteen. Much of the time I was at boarding school so in some respects my memories of Henbury are a bit fragmentary.

In the early days of the war, we left Hill End as I explained above, never to return. When the RAF relinquished the house at the end of the war, I was away abroad in the Royal Marines, one of my sisters was at College soon to qualify as a teacher, and my younger sister, Sarah Jean was not very well. Eventually a year or two later when she was about fifteen, she was diagnosed with MS. She died when she was about thirty which was sad for all concerned. She was loved and looked after by all the family but being bedridden so early she had no youth to speak of.

My parents did not want to return to Hill End which no doubt had deteriorated, and perhaps held too many memories for them. When the Nuns wanted to buy it, they were pleased to sell it to them. As you know, there is little recognizable left in that neighbourhood now.

After the war, John James's parents moved to Heneage Court in Gloucestershire. Much later they moved to Sheepwood, near Bristol.

Andrew Painter's family keep in close contact with their former employer's family, evidence that country employer-employee relationships are often built on great mutual regard. John James's sister Mrs Pamela Sykes writes,

I was born Pam James, and lived at Hill End Henbury for the first ten years of my life. Pam Sims' mother Mrs Minnie Painter was the much-loved Nanny of my younger sister and myself. We loved her from the first moment that she arrived, and I have kept in touch ever since, as has my brother. Life was so much simpler then. From a very young age, we were taken for long walks every day. Often it was across the local fields and woods, but if the pram was involved, we might go all the way to Westbury by roads, through 'our' village, splashing through the ford (Sampson Way's big house on the right), then the Salutation Inn, up Henbury hill, down the other side – looking back, it does seem a long way for two very little girls, but we thought nothing of it. Another walk was 'The Brentry Round' via the railway bridge and past the (Old?) Crow, and there were days in Blaise woods … later, we explored further on ponies under the care of Andrew Painter – Minnie's husband-to-be.

Trinmore, Clifton Down. Arthur Albert Levy Langfield and family

The Langfield Family of Henbury Court Dower House

Mr A.A. Levy Langfield was a Bristol City Councillor from 1896 to 1913, and Alderman between 1913 and 1927, following closely in his father's footsteps. He was also a Docks Member who declined to pledge himself to the concept of the Royal Edward Dock in 1901 when 70 council members voted in favour. According to his family he was his own man, unafraid to stand alone when he thought it necessary. The *Western Daily Press* described him as in general, good-tempered and of shrewd judgement, and with exceptional business capacity and initiative. He also had philanthropic interests.

Mr Langfield was by profession a draper of Levy Langfield and Co. with premises in Bridge Street in the City of Bristol. The family home was at Trinmore on Clifton Down, where his children grew up. He also owned land and property in Henbury. Mr Robert Biggs of The Elms Dairy Farm remembered that his grandfather Stanley Biggs took up the tenancy of his farm from Mr Langfield early in the twentieth century. Then in about 1920 Mr Gunn of Henbury House bought the farmland and Stan himself bought the farmhouse from the owner.

Henbury Court, when it became a hotel, was co-owned by Sir Thomas Lennard and Mr Levy Langfield. After the war, it was, like the farms, compulsorily purchased by Bristol City Council for housing development at a derisory price. Harold Godfrey recalls that several of the Botany Bay Cottages were also owned by Mr Langfield.

However, it wasn't until 1939 that part of the family came to live in Henbury. This was Mr Levy Langfield's son Alexander. His younger son Paul writes,

My father Alexander G.L. Langfield moved with his wife Molly into the Dower House at the outbreak of the Second World War. Their son

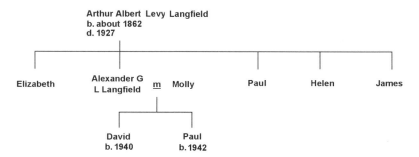

High-Class Family & Residential Hotel
Delightfully Situated in its Own Grounds of 27 Acres.

David and Paul in Henbury Court Garden
and, *below*, in Blaise Castle estate

David was born in March 1940 and Paul in August 1942. Our maid Edith Hammond arrived in 1942.

I remember Henbury as a delightful village/hamlet – the bluebells in May and the many varieties of butterfly in the summer in the fields towards Hallen. I remember exploring Henbury Court with my brother, looking for newts, tadpoles, water boatmen in the ornamental pond in Henbury Court. During the severe winter of 1947 my father actually skied to work at the Bristol Aeroplane Company's Filton Plant.

In 1947 Henbury Court was compulsorily purchased – twenty seven acres for just £10,000.

In the fifties it was decided to build a road through the middle of our garden, my father learning of this in the evening paper. As the estates were built in Henbury in the middle fifties, my parents decided to move, and we left I think in 1957. We moved to Rockleaze in Sneyd Park where we were nearer to Clifton College where my brother and I were both pupils.

I cannot think of a nicer place than Henbury to have spent my boyhood years.

7

Families involved in business and trade in Henbury village centre:
Newman, Harvey and Grigg

Unlike neighbouring Westbury on Trym, Henbury had not in living memory had a large business and trading centre. However, until after World War II, a small number of such facilities had existed in the main village street that led to the gate of Blaise Castle Estate. There was the house and office of the Clerk to the Magistrates, a plumber and taxi service, a Post Office, a small general store, the Porter Store, and also, until just before the war, a blacksmith, a cobbler and a sweet shop. These provided the day to day basics so essential to a fairly isolated small community.

The Newman Family

Charles Newman, a Devonshire schoolmaster, and his wife Annie, had four daughters and four sons. The eldest named after his father would as a child help to boost the family economy by digging the vegetable garden and catching trout with bare hands in the stream. When he was about twelve years old, he was noticed by the local squire who wanted Charles to catalogue his library, for which the reward was an occasional golden sovereign.

Charles Alfred was an avid reader and worked hard at his studies, borrowing books and regularly walking some miles to obtain coaching before starting life as a pupil teacher in Wiltshire. In about 1885 he journeyed to Henbury to take up a teaching post at Henbury Boys School when the Headmaster was Mr Higgs. Charles lodged at Rose Bank with a Mr and Mrs Thomas Howe.

One of Charles's descendants writes,

> Mrs Howe who was born Catherine Pettit first came to live in Henbury in the late 1860s when she worked as a children's nurse for Dr George Archer and his family. The Archers moved from Canterbury to live at Chesterfield House. (Catherine herself came from a Kentish village.) When she married Thomas Howe, they went to live at Rose Bank,

The Newman Family tree

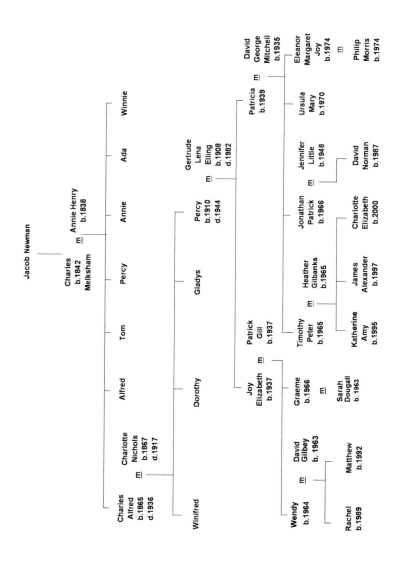

Charles Alfred

Charlotte

opposite the village entrance to the Blaise Castle Estate.

Catherine had a sister Charlotte who suffered a long period of ill health before an early death. Her husband Samuel Nichols had four young children to care for as well as his wife. It was then arranged that his daughter Charlotte should live with her Aunt Catherine for a time. At Rose Bank, Charles and Charlotte became friends and gradually fell in love. They married in 1893, and set up home in Raglan Villa in the heart of the village, and there they brought up their three daughters and after a gap of years their son.

Charles did not remain in his teaching post but by enterprise and industry took on a number of interesting and useful duties. His daughter Dorothy writes,

Hearing that the 'Parish Clerk Assistant Overseer and Rate Collector' (all one job) had died, he walked some miles to ask the Chairman of the Parish Council to support him in obtaining this appointment. He refused, saying he had someone else in mind. Typically, Charles then walked many miles more to ask all the other Council members for their support. On the day of the decision, all the votes except one were given to him.

From this he got on, becoming also secretary to various funds and charities. Some called him 'Father Confessor of the Parish'. Many came to him in trouble and in joy or for his advice or help. He had a good business head, and made wills for many, helped with their income tax forms etc.

Older Henbury residents also remember that he was Clerk to Henbury Magistrates Court sited next to the Police Station in Hallen Road.

From his early days in the village, he made many friends among all social levels. He knew his way round the farms and hamlets. Dorothy Newman describes another encounter of her father's:

> At the outbreak of war, representatives of the War Office arrived from London having been informed that he was the man who knew as well as anyone about the surrounding country. They had come to requisition land and some houses and cottages for essential war work.

Charles found himself trying to act in the best interest of both officialdom and his neighbours. He must have succeeded for his daughter writes that after the war ended, he was invited to a reception at the Salutation Inn:

> To his great surprise and emotion, a big assembly of all classes of men were there to make him a presentation in gratitude for all his service over their cause. They said, 'Most people say beautiful things about the dead, but we want to try to say it while you are alive.'

> He loved all living creatures, people and animals. One of his hobbies was breeding Chinchilla rabbits. He won medals for honey and wax from his bees. He enjoyed wood carving and rock-gardening. He wrote articles about country things – rare flowers and birds etc. and had them published.

Dorothy remembers that it was through her father that the Henbury Flower Show started.

> When the family first had Raglan Villa, it had only a flower garden in front and a yard at the back, but one day, Charles came home with great joy, gathered his family round him, and said that he had bought the big garden, orchard and nuttery at the back of the house. He said he would have a door made in the dividing wall. Charlotte said she couldn't wait so Charles fetched a ladder, and they all climbed over the wall to inspect their new acquisition.

Dorothy continues,

> It was a lovely garden all planted and in order with lush fruit, apple and pear trees, a tall walnut tree and lots of hazel nut trees; and beyond them, now where Battersby Way lies, a tennis court and orchard. Later on, a field was added. It was great fun, and mother was like a little child as she planned a part for fowls etcetera.

Charlotte lived to enjoy her garden until she was forty-nine years old, when to her family's great grief she died. After her untimely death, Charles and his children found that their joy in the garden was shrouded.

Dorothy Newman, who became a Carmelite Sister in Birmingham and later in Oban, was born in 1896. In the quietness of her convent, she wrote down her memories of her father and mother and her family. She describes a very early memory,

> As a child, I remember on a walk with Dad through the fields, a very surly-looking man barred the way over a style. He was sucking an empty clay pipe. Dad brought out his tobacco pouch, and said, 'Fill up, and press it well down with your thumb.' Then he lit up the man's pipe for him. I was struck by the change in the man's face as he stepped aside for us to get over the stile.

Dorothy mentions that whenever her father had to be away on business, he would bring a present of another pet. They loved birds, and had a room in the house with a tree and nests, and canaries and other birds. The pigeons were out of doors of course. When Charles went to North Devon, he would take a homing pigeon, and tie a letter under its wings. All the way from Ilfracombe the bird would fly home to Henbury – and Charlotte and the family would welcome it back.

Dorothy remembers her father was 'kind, but could be stern, on occasions such as the reading of a school report.'

Later, in his old age, long after the death of his wife, his leg was amputated. He had a nurse to look after him, and a devoted housekeeper, Violet Miller. To enable him to go down into the tennis court on his own, he had a rail erected. He would sit very still with the country life, which he so loved, all around, and the very wild birds even would fly down and eat out of his hands.

In the end, his death was sudden. Gladys and Percy spent that night in sorrow. Early next morning, through the open window, Gladys heard men going to their work, and one said to the other, 'That was where he lived. He was a good man, if ever there was one.'

Percy Newman, son of Charles and Charlotte
Dorothy, writing many years later, recalled many incidents in the life of her young brother.

> Percy was born some time after his three sisters. There was much discussion about the name of this new baby. Eventually Charles declared 'He shall be named Percy after my youngest brother, and no other name.' His mother Charlotte died when he was only seven years old. The little boy was then mothered by his eldest sister Winnie who also then kept house for the family.

Percy had many friends, and hobbies. At one time as a small boy he set up an enterprise selling rabbits – an idea frowned upon by his father. He started school at St.Ursula's Convent, later progressing to Bristol Grammar School. Dorothy says, 'he did not have a scholarly bent, but he knew the workings and makes and models of all motor bikes by their sound!' He eventually enlisted Dorothy's help to ask their father if he could have a motor-bike to ride to school on. She notes that he had numerous accidents on bikes, and later on in 'bangers' too:

> On one occasion, Percy had appendicitis. Now, as a small boy he was in a prime position to reach the village sweetshop – next door, in fact. As the ambulance waited at the gates, and all the family stood by anxiously and solemnly, Mr Windsor came running from his shop, and, stopping the ambulance, pressed some bags into father's hands – all Percy's favourite sweets to comfort him!

> One of his holidays was at the Duke of York's Camp where children from all kinds of school camped together. He had a strenuous time, and reported that the Prince of Wales and the Duke of York were very jolly – the soon-to-be Edward VIII and George VI.

Percy

Arthur Newman, our cousin, came to live with us after his father's death. The two boys each had an attic for a bedroom with a landing in between. They fixed up a telephone, and were very proud of their contrivance despite the fact that even without it they could still hear each other!

Percy was very friendly with the Farr family at Brentry Lodge. Their daughter Edna was about his age. They lent him their cottage for weekends, at Severn Beach, which in those days was a wild stretch of stones and grass for miles – and only a cottage here and there. He took his tent on these occasions. When the Farr family joined him, they would go out in the early morning to some lobster pots, and find shrimps. There was a cottage nearby which belonged to a man they called 'Shrimpy Willie' because he had a boiler, and would cook shrimps on it, and sell them for a 'penny a poke' (bagful).

Percy grew up in this happy environment, and in course of time he fell in love, and married Lena Elling, a daughter of Mr and Mrs Elling of Westbury on Trym. The young couple lived in a small house before moving to the family home at Raglan Villa. They had two daughters, Joy and Pat. Shortly after this the war started, and in spite of being in a 'reserved occupation' (the Inland Revenue), he enlisted in the R.A.F., and with his crew was shot down and killed over Germany in 1944.

Two small girls were left fatherless, at almost the same ages that Percy himself had been left motherless. Lena their mother eventually moved her family back to Westbury where she had grown up. Dorothy's two sisters left their family home to marry, and to bring up families of their own. Three generations of the Newman family lived in Henbury, well-liked and respected by other villagers and much missed at their final departure.

Harvey Family of Henbury Road

The Harveys had lived at the centre of Henbury village since the 1860s. They originated from Bridgwater in Somerset with ancestry known to have gone back to Devon landowners. Henry Harvey born 1833 in Bath, moved in the 1850s to Ebbw Vale, Wales in search of building work following a building boom as new industries developed. He married Mary J. of Melksham born 1834. They had two sons born at Ebbw Vale, Thomas Henry and Frederick T. Then in the early 1860s, they moved to Westbury on Trym where in 1866 their son Frank was born. Two years later, another son John was born in Henbury followed by two more children, Herbert and Annie.

The 1881 census shows Henry, plumber and painter, as Head of the family employing four men and two boys. His eldest son Thomas, occupation 'Plumber,' and Fred 'Painter and Decorator'; Frank was 'Apprentice Plumber'. At that time, the other children were 'scholars'.

In the census of 1891, Frederick is Head of family, his wife Elizabeth was born in Bridgwater, and they have three children, Ellen M, Henry George and Herbert E. Frederick puts his occupation as 'Plumber'.

Some interesting information came to light about Thomas in an article by Judith Green. Thomas, Frederick's elder brother (Tom), met Lizzie Ogborne when they were both members of St Mary's Church choir. They fell in love, but Lizzie's parents wanted her to follow the family custom of marrying a farmer. However, Tom the Plumber was ambitious, and wanted to become a landed gentleman, and 'found' a dynasty of his own. Tom promised Lizzie a farm in Australia much bigger and better than any farm the Ogbornes ever had.

They married at St Mary's in October in 1881, and sailed away from Plymouth to Sydney. They experienced a mixed fortune there, land at that time being difficult to acquire. However, Tom's plumbing

H. W. HARVEY,

PLUMBER, GLAZIER, PAINTER,
GENERAL HOUSE CONTRACTOR,
AND SANITARY ENGINEER.

HENBURY VILLAGE, Near BRISTOL.

———

ESTIMATES GIVEN FOR REPAIRS.

The Harvey Family tree

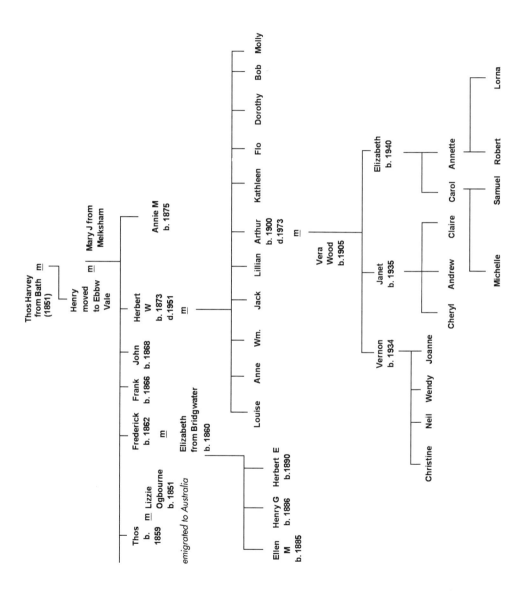

Three generations of Harveys

business thrived, and over the years became 'Harvey Industries'. Tom and Lizzie had nine children, but sadly she died before Tom acquired his 1,000 acre farm, which they named 'Redlands'; but for a time it was run by her second son.

Back in Henbury, it seems to have been Frederick's younger brother Herbert, born 1873, who eventually kept the family plumbing business going with his son Arthur who was a close friend to Ray McEwen Smith of Westmoreland Farm. The many skills and services provided by this versatile family are well-remembered and well-regarded by older residents. Over the years they carried out contractual work on many of the big houses, as well as keeping the taxi services and general plumbing business in being.

Arthur

In 1933 Arthur, born 1900, married Vera Blanche Wood from Sevenhampton in the Cotswolds. The young couple moved to a house in Fishpool Hill (a road that led into Charlton village). It was one of several houses recently built that they rented from Mr Raines who also owned Drew's Stores in Westbury Village. The couple eventually bought the property from him. Arthur continued to run the family business, and he

Harvey House and business premises

The house faces the gates into Blaise Castle Estate

Arthur Harvey with parrot

and Vera still regarded themselves as part of Henbury in those rural times, when Brentry was a mere hamlet. Arthur continued to see his boyhood friends in their old haunts – inns, skittles etc. They continued to go to St. Mary's Henbury. When their three children Vernon, Janet and Elizabeth reached school age they attended the Henbury Schools. When Vernon and Janet were there the boys' and girls' schools were church elementary schools, so Janet remained there until she reached fourteen. However Vernon, at eleven years old, passed exams for Chipping Sodbury

Success! Arthur Harvey and friends with the Severnside Skittles League Trophy

Grammar School. When Elizabeth reached eleven the system was changing and the Henbury Schools were closing – she had to attend Filton
Secondary School, which entailed a substantial daily cycle ride. Here she
did a secretarial course.

After leaving school, Elizabeth went to work in the office of Arcade
Sewing Machines. Janet worked in an office too, and Vernon first went to
work for HH Budgett and Co Ltd. Later he joined a cash and carry company. Then, later, Elizabeth joined a national cash and carry company
where she became their first female manager.

All three of them married and had children. When her children were older,
Elizabeth went to work for the same company as her brother. She brought
her girls up in Nailsea where they attended Nailsea School. Carol went to
work for cash and carry after leaving School, and Annette worked as a
nurse at Brentry Hospital, Bristol.

Arthur continued the Henbury plumbing business with his father Herbert
until Herbert's death in 1951. After that Arthur continued running the
business from his own home.

The village street. The horse and trap is just passing the blacksmith's shop on the right of the picture

Grigg family of Henbury Road, in the heart of the village

One of the most essential services in a rural area before the war was that of the blacksmith. The tasks included shoeing horses and repairing farm machinery. In Henbury in those days, John Grigg's smithy was a bright, noisy ever-busy fascinating place. I count it as a failure that it has not been possible to trace his family to include it in this study. However what I have been able to include is a copy of the entry in the census of 1881. From this, one learns that John and his wife Amelia were both born in Cornwall, John in Wadebridge and his wife in nearby Egloshayle. For many years, John was blacksmith in the heart of Henbury Village opposite the Porter Stores

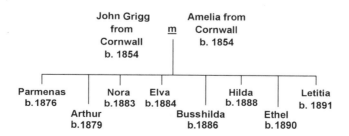

and next door to the Post Office where John Warburton worked and brought up his family.

The furnace, and the smells and hammering fascinated the young Henbury boys as they watched horses being led under the lintel of the blacksmith's shop to be shod.

The smithy in its modern incarnation has been beautifully restored and incorporated into the house by the present owner.

The Griggs left the village not long before the outbreak of World War II.

Roy Pearce remembers that Parmenas Grigg, or his son, had a blacksmith's shop in part of the old College building in Westbury. Roy believes that at some later date, Grigg moved his smithy to the High Street near to Mealings smithy.

8

The Powesland family

Peter Powesland is important to Henbury because he kept records and was secretary to a number of local charities, some of which had been administered by Charles Newman in his day. He also knew many Henbury people and their families and was a great source of information to any who wished to know about the village when it was truly 'rural'. He knew about the houses and their history, and was generous in imparting his knowledge. In writing the three Henbury books, I personally owe a great deal to him, not only for his encouragement but also for his critical appraisal! He was after all a Senior Lecturer at Bristol University. His friends miss him, but they will never forget him. It is fitting that this last chapter should be devoted to Peter and his family.

In 1928 Francis Powesland, his wife Ada Blanche and their three small children moved to Henbury with Dr Wills. Dr Wills had bought the Vicarage, recently vacated by the last of the Way clerical family. Francis – known to his friends as Frank – was employed by Dr Wills as his chauffeur, and the good doctor offered Frank the garden flat in the old Vicarage to accommodate the family. In the following year, their second son Peter Francis Powesland made his appearance. The garden flat was then thought to be too small for the expanding family, so Dr Wills arranged an exchange with his gardener who lived with his wife at number two Elm Cottages. Peter always looked back with affection at the Old Vicarage, the place of his birth.

Of the four Powesland children, the eldest child Philip died as a young man, and Pamela and Patricia married and left the village. After a number of years in the R.A.F. and in Canada, Peter returned to Henbury where he spent the rest of his life.

Peter's sister Patricia writes a little more detail about her family:

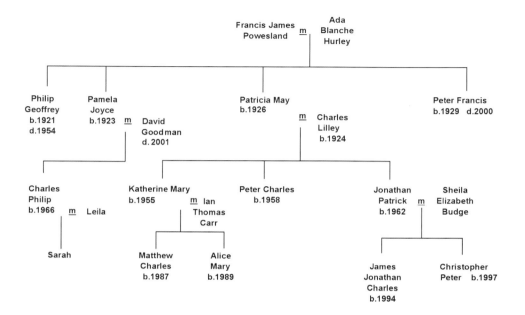

After he left Cotham Grammar school, Philip worked as a clerk at Avonmouth Docks where he was hugely interested in the many ships that came and went in those days. War broke out when he was eighteen, and he was called up into the Army. He spent a long time in the Middle East with the Royal Army Ordnance Corps. When war ended he went to Bristol University graduating in Economics. He then spent some years in Uganda as a University lecturer. Sadly he died when he was only thirty-three.

My sister Pamela and I left home long before we married. Pamela graduated from Bristol University and worked for the Foreign Office, and later for the United Nations in New York and Geneva. She lives near Geneva.

I joined BOAC (whose H.Q. came to Bristol at the outbreak of war) when I left school, and later worked for them in London and a number of other places before finishing up with three years in Hong Kong. There I met a handsome young R.A.F. officer, and we were married in St Mary's Church Henbury in June 1952. We celebrated our Golden

Francis and Ada Blanche Powesland and their children.
A photograph probably taken in 1933

Peter Powesland

wedding anniversary last year.

I would like to add a few words about my mother. She was always a great source of support and encouragement to all of us in our various endeavours. There are probably still a few people around who would remember her as a faithful member of the Mothers' Union and the Women's Institute.

My mother's family all lived in Bristol but originated from Stogumber in Somerset. My father's father was a soldier, and presumably the family moved around a lot. But Dad was a complete orphan while still a youngster, and seems to have been farmed out to various relatives.

From conversations with Peter some years ago the following information emerged about his younger days. He started school at Henbury Boys School next to the church. He made many friends some of whom he kept in touch with through his adult life. Peter Michael Baguley was the son of Sexton Harry Baguley, and they lived at Sexton's Cottage. Peter said that the two Peters played in the churchyard (regarded by his friend as his garden) sometimes noisily. Frank discouraged this, but most of the time, their playground was Blaise woods where they could climb trees, play hide and seek and games of make-believe. As a young boy, his companions were mainly the children of fathers employed at the large houses, such as Ronnie Clifford and Eddie Shepherd. The child population in Henbury was not large in those days, many pupils came from outlying villages and farms. So there were plenty of friends in school time but not so many in out-of-school time. Another source of friends was membership of St Mary's choir. He loved singing, and music remained a great joy and interest throughout his life. He kept in touch throughout his life with a few of these early childhood friends. One of these was his friend Peter Baguley. When Peter Francis Powesland went to Cotham Grammar School, Peter Michael Baguley went to Technical School. (In his adult life he became a B.B.C. journalist.)

Peter was ten years old when war started. At eleven years old, he won a scholarship to Cotham Grammar School. As each of the Powesland children reached eleven, they won scholarships to Bristol secondary schools. Each morning, they would walk into Westbury to pick up the bus into town. By 1938 there was a regular 40 minute bus service between the city and Romneys Garage (corner of Cribbs Causeway and Station Road) now long demolished. The tram service ceased about this time too. Peter widened his circle of friends as a result of changing schools and because he could travel further afield.

Peter remembered annual holidays when Dr Wills loaned one of his cars to Frank for the occasion. He enjoyed attending the Hallen and Henbury

Flower Show on the Show Ground by the ford, and the horse show held in a field opposite Botany Bay Cottages. He admitted to being wistful when he watched children his own age competing in the 'events'. To be a child in wartime had its excitements for Peter. First, an Anderson Air Raid Shelter was built in their garden, much used during the winter of 1940. Then his father became an air raid warden and took his share of duties round the village. On one occasion, Cotham School was damaged in a raid, and the boys had to join Fairfield Grammar School for a day. Some time later, the Anderson shelter became water-logged and damp, and Major Sampson Way, who was now senior warden, came to the family's rescue, and invited them to use his cellars. Peter had only one fear on those occasions, because the Sampson Way dog, named Blotto, guarded the dining room door, and had to be passed en route to the lavatory.

The evacuation of British schoolchildren was in principle a good idea. However, in the haste, and with lack of experience in dealing with a large number of children in such a way, mismatches were made. Unfortunately for him, Peter was mismatched to his hosts in Cheltenham. To his great relief, he was allowed to return home.

By the thirties, most of the food basics were delivered to the door from Westbury, and dairy produce from The Elms Dairy farm, originally by horse-drawn vans, but in his childhood they were mechanized. The family used Henbury Post Office and occasionally the village store.

Peter took his School Certificate in 1944, and went into the sixth form. After that he worked for an insurance company until he was called up for National Service 1947-1949 with the R.A.F. He worked there as a Personnel Selection clerk. He was then selected and took a short-service commission in the R.A.F. for seven years until 1954. The psychological testing he had been trained to do stood him in good stead, for he won a city senior scholarship to Bristol University where he read philosophy and psychology. After graduating with a first class degree, he took up a one year resident Fellowship at Queen's University in Canada where he was awarded an M.A.

In 1958 he returned to Bristol University as 'Demonstrator/Researcher' and Lecturer. He lived for some time in one of the University Halls of Residence as Warden.

Patricia recalls,

> When our mother died in 1963 he returned to Elm Cottages, partly to keep Dad company and partly to help him out. He became a senior lecturer at the University, and later acting head of Department for four years until his retirement. When Dr Wills died, he had left number Two Elm Cottages to Frank. On Dad's death Peter bought our share of the house from me and my sister, and there he lived and eventually died.

He will surely be remembered for many years in Henbury and far beyond.

Finale

In 1986 we left Westbury on Trym and bought Old Westmoreland farm-house in preparation for our retirement. This move made so great an impact upon us that it inspired three books about Henbury Village in its rural days.

The appearance and atmosphere of the old house was immediately intriguing, stone built from about the late sixteenth-century, it has low beamed ceilings and thick walls. Inset in the walls were pieces of wood probably once lintels of earlier doors and windows because the stonework shows that the house had elongated over the centuries, from one-up one-down (Keeper's Cottage-cum-animal byre). Then a storey was added to the byre to extend the living accommodation, and so on, until it became three-up three-down – and two large byres and a barn.

Shortly after moving in we met our neighbours Farmer Ray and his wife Vivienne who lived in the newer (early nineteenth-century) wing of the farmhouse. It had been built at right angles to the older part and contained much higher ceilings. We received a heartfelt welcome and, before long, we all became good friends.

The initial impact the house made on us was soon heightened by learning about the farm that underlay it, and the career of Ray its farmer. His story had so many elements to it – tragedy, deep happiness, great endeavour and above all love of his job.

When we first met him Ray was an old and somewhat reticent man, a dour figure in our eyes. On further acquaintance he turned out to be truly kind and at times very funny. He also exhibited exemplary patience when for instance asked repeatedly for details of his farming days. His patience was born of the pleasure he found in recalling happy memories.

'But,' he said, 'to find out more about farming in Henbury, you must consult Tom Hignell and Robert Biggs, and then go and talk to Peter Powesland who looks after village trusts and charities – he knows as much about Henbury's history and also knows a lot of older residents who can remember the village in pre-war rural days.'

This all led to meeting very many more local people, until a picture started to emerge of a village nucleus now almost surrounded by new housing. When it was collected together, Peter said 'what a mass of facts! Now make it readable!' When I did just that, it turned into three small books, all of which I hope are readable!

For me, the benefits of discovering Henbury as it was in the years leading up to World War II are that it has given me enormous pleasure. The atmosphere I first sensed in our house and also in the village with all its remaining fields, hedges and watercourses, is now explained by getting to know those who have lived contented lives here. Everyone interviewed said their lives had been happy in Henbury.

An impression given by contributors is of orderly lives influenced to some extent by a hierarchical society. Most were church going families, the church providing for both religious and social activities.

It should not, however, be assumed that the residents were all perfect. This village had its normal share of human weakness, for instance some were prone to gambling, there were young men's fights, probably when the ale flowed freely of a Saturday night. An occasional baby was born out of, or only just within, holy wedlock. The Magistrates' Court in Hallen Road dealt with small crimes and misdemeanours. Next door in the Police house, Sergeant Harding provided a strong presence on behalf of the Law to discourage would-be miscreants.

Mr Baker wrote to the Vicar complaining that there was poor attendance at early Sunday Communion services – I for one have sympathy with those lie-a-beds after those six long days of a relentless working week.

My conclusion is that our early instinctive feelings towards Henbury have been strongly confirmed as a result of our researches. Henbury village was a very human, kindly place. In the structure of its society it was, by the time World War II broke out, just emerging from Victorian values and lifestyles.

By general consent a very good place in which to grow up.

Map reference by chapter

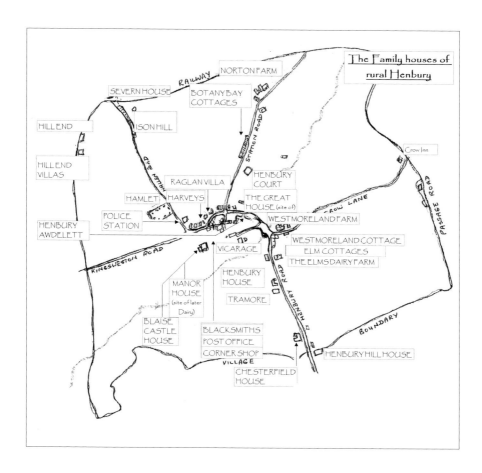

The Family houses of rural Henbury

NORTON FARM
SEVERN HOUSE
RAILWAY
BOTANY BAY COTTAGES
HILL END
ISON HILL
HILL END VILLAS
STATION ROAD
Crow Inn
HENBURY COURT
RAGLAN VILLA
THE GREAT HOUSE (site of)
HAMLET HARVEYS
CROW LANE
PASSAGE ROAD
POLICE STATION
WESTMORELAND FARM
HENBURY AWDELETT
WESTMORELAND COTTAGE
ELM COTTAGES
THE ELMS DAIRY FARM
KINGSWESTON ROAD
VICARAGE
HENBURY ROAD
HENBURY HOUSE
MANOR HOUSE (site of later Dairy)
TRAMORE
BOUNDARY
BLAISE CASTLE HOUSE
BLACKSMITHS
POST OFFICE
CORNER SHOP
VILLAGE
HENBURY HILL HOUSE
CHESTERFIELD HOUSE

Acknowledgements

This book has been largely written by members of the families included here, and edited by me, the writer. The task would have been extremely difficult without the help of our son Philip who has spent many hours arranging the 'trees' and pre-editing the text before sending to the publisher. I give my thanks to him and to three of our grandchildren, Rebecca, Emma and Alexander, for their encouragement and help in tackling the computer! Many thanks are due too to Mr John Sansom of Redcliffe Press for the excellent way he has presented the three books.

My grateful thanks are here recorded to the following contributors:

Aldridge
Miss Elizabeth Osborn
Mr Mark Osborn
Mrs Joan Tribe
Mrs Susan Townsend

Baker
Mr David Culliford
Mr Peter Powesland

Biggs
Mr Roy Pearce
Mr Victor Goodfield
Mr R Biggs
Mr John Roberts

Budgett
Mrs Julie Bate

Clifford
Mrs Ruby Clifford
Mr Stanley Clifford
Mr Ronald Clifford

Cox
Mrs Shirley Meaden (née Cox)

Godfrey
Mr Harold Godfrey

Goodfield
Mr Victor Goodfield

Grigg
Census Return
Mr Roy Pearce

Gunn
Miss Diana Gunn
Mr Brian Gunn
Mr James Gunn

Harford
Mr Richard Hill

Harvey
Mrs Elizabeth Amos (née Harvey)
Mr Vernon Harvey

Hignell

Mr Tom Hignell

Mrs Eunice Rodda

James

Mr John James

Mrs Pamela Sykes (née James)

Lane

Mr Ken Lane

Langfield

Mr Paul Langfield

Love

Mrs Beryl Hill (née Love)

Mr Dennis Love

Newman

Mrs Patricia Mitchell (née Newman)

Painter

Mrs Pamela Sims (née Painter)

Powesland

Mr Peter Powesland

Mrs Patricia Lilley (née Powesland)

Steer

Mr Bob Steer

Way

Mrs Abigail Moat (née Way)

Woodsford/Talbot

Mrs Betty Talbot (née Woodsford)

Mr Fred Talbot

Warburton

Mr David Hellen

Mrs Pauline Stevenson

Sources

Thanks are due to the authors, editors and publishers of a number of publications as follows:

Bristol Channel Guide, edited by L. Langfield

Baker, *Obituaries*, courtesy of D. Culliford

Burke's Peerage

Eveleigh D., *A Popular Retreat*, City of Bristol Museum and Art Gallery & Kingswood Press 1987

Green J., 'Australia Bound – Three Families from Bristol', from an article published by Bristol and Avon Family History Society, June 2002

Hallen and Henbury Women's Institute, *A Guide to Henbury*, 1970, Bailey & Son Ltd, Dursley

Harford A. *The Annals of the Harford Family* (edited 1909)

Newman D., Unpublished memoirs of the Newman Family, courtesy of P. Mitchell

Powesland P., Unpublished documents and notes, courtesy of D. Culliford

Rudder S., *A New History of Gloucestershire*, first published 1777

St Mary's Church Henbury, Graveyard

St Mary's Church leaflet, *A Brief History*

Way Revd C.P., *Henbury Vicarage 1830-1927*

Wilkins Revd H.J., *Ecclesiastical History of Westbury on Trym*, J. Arrowsmith Bristol & London, 1909